NATURAL MYSTIC

Down To Earth & Spiritual

NATURAL MYSTIC

Down To Earth & Spiritual

NICOLA RICHARDSON

NATURAL MYSTIC
Down to Earth & Spiritual
E-Book Available

'Tune in' and Download the Playlist of Natural Mystic

@nicolarich_words

FOR **ROB & DYLAN**
Forever grateful.

Author's Note for the Second Edition

When I first wrote *Natural Mystic*, I could never have imagined the quiet journey it would take, not only into the hearts of readers, but around the world.
Over the years, I've been deeply touched to hear from readers as far afield as Australia, the Middle East, and beyond, who have found something comforting and familiar in these pages.

One very special copy even went on tour with the legendary band Simply Red, who were kind enough to sign it for me. Later, I had the pleasure of meeting Nightmares on Wax, another artist whose music is part of the accompanying playlist, and he too generously signed a copy.

These artists are just a few of the names mentioned in the soundtrack interwoven with this book, a playlist that reflects the rhythm, spirit, and soulful heart of *Natural Mystic*. And who knows, perhaps I'll continue to gather more signatures as this little book quietly travels into new hands.

Wherever you are reading this, whether you are returning or opening it for the first time, I hope this new second edition brings you calm, connection, and the courage to trust your own wisdom.

With love,
Nic

First published in Great Britain in 2019 by Daisa & Co

Copyright © 2019 by NICOLA RICHARDSON

The moral right of the Author has been asserted.

All rights reserved. No part of this publication may be reproduced, stored in a retrieval system, transmitted, or copied in any form or by any means, electronic, mechanical, photocopying, recording or otherwise, without the prior written permission of the publisher and copyright owner.

The information given in this book should not be treated as a substitute as professional advice. Any use of information in this book is at the reader's discretion and risk. Neither the author nor the publisher can be held responsible for any loss, claim or damage arising out of the use, or misuse, of the suggestions made or for any material on third party websites.
The editors have ensured a true reflection of the author's tone and voice has remained present throughout. This book is a work of non-fiction based on the true life recollections and experiences of the author. The author wishes to express her apologies for any unintentional embarrassment or offence caused and wishes to express her deepest respect for all mentioned.

A CIP catalogue record for this book is available from the British Library.

Printed in England

Contents

Dedication	iv
Contents	vi
Introduction	x
Acknowledgements	xi

Part I - Foundation	
To Begin…	1
A Sagittarian is Born	3
1976	6
Genuine	9
West Street, My Happy Place	11
The Pub	19
D.I.V.O.R.C.E	21
Chaotic Lifestyle & Addiction	26
Part II - Exploration	
Life as a Teenager	31
Raving	37
Nanny Eva	39
Words of Wisdom	40
Globe Trotting	45
Going Solo	48
New Year's Eve 1999	52
Thailand & Vietnam	55

Part III - Belonging
Mr. Rich 59
Journey of Development 65
Counselling 70
Meditation 73
Colour Therapy & Chakras 76
Reiki 78

Part IV – Becoming
Marriage 84
999 87
Corby 89
Anxiety & Panic Attacks 91
Dylan Oliver 93
No Fixed Abode 95
A Decade 99

Part V – Seeking
My Spirit Guide – Red Mountain 101
Route 66 110
Dowsing 113
One Very Lucky Cat 116
Fall Out 118
How Did My Spirituality Develop? 119
Connection 126
Messages Received 129
Messages Given 133
Automatic Writing 141
Psychic Fayres 145
Temping Again 148
Life Coaching 150
Red Mountain Wellbeing 155
Care & Support 161
Meditation & Brain Injury 165

NHS	167
Community Work	169
'Getting people back to work'	170
Meditation for Job Seekers & Learning Disabilities	173
Concussion & Whiplash	175
Life as an Office Temp	180
Working 9-5 as a Sensitive/Empath	185

Part VI - Wisdom

Court case	190
Publishing	198
Nicola Wisdom	201
Waiting for the Sentence	204
Closure	207
Open Letters	211

Part VII - Empowerment

The Future	214
Guidance	219

"I will always guide you, look to no other, other than your own inner soul and wisdom."

-Red Mountain

So, here I am...

I'm finally piecing together all the journals I have been keeping for the last 4 years, as my journey of development has unfolded; following the guidance I have received.

I am now 40, and as I have been explaining, to my very good friend Emma, it is the beginning of a new chapter, a new decade.

On 22nd April 2013, to begin my journal, I spoke three affirmations, to stop focusing on the reward and to enjoy the journey...

1. I live in excited anticipation to see how the universe will surprise me.
2. I give value to my clients - they value my work and they reward me appropriately.
3. I earn a good living for my meaningful work.

My Spirit Guide has said to me...

"As you enter your 40's your wisdom will grow. You will need to stand in your own shadow, and not that of another. You have your own story to write, you are not a consequence of someone else's story. Create your light and allow yourself to shine.

No need to challenge – no need to prove you are right. Just follow your destiny.

I will always guide you – look to no other, other than your own inner soul and wisdom."

I had been working for myself; teaching and training people to Meditate and bring Mindfulness into their daily lives. My main objective was to demystify the ideas and theories that people, clients and service providers had. I wanted to create a credible service that helped people. I absolutely loved what I was doing with a passion, and I was very sad and heartbroken when this ended. I loved the simple fact that I was free to be creative with my work. It was up to me to work out the programs - adjusting and changing as necessary. There were no silly rules. I was free to be me and wear the clothes that I wanted to. I have a big need to have my feet free and sometimes sandals are the only option for me.

Unfortunately, circumstances sucker-punched me in the solar plexus and this is where and how I landed in HR.

So, I found myself in a HR role and had been trying to decide whether I could actually 'make a proper go of it'. Wondering if this is just the job I needed to get me started on a 'proper' career path. I had been so torn, because I know in my sensible head, if I applied myself and made a commitment, I could develop in this new role.

But my heart and soul were telling me that I had a book to write. This book had been a long time in the making; I guess life just gets in the way sometimes.

No… Rewind and start again. It certainly does get in the way sometimes.

My guide told me that I would find this job. He told me what to expect from the interview and he told me what salary I would get. He also told me that this role would bridge the gap to allow me to get the book finished!

I'm not sure if it came across in the interview, but I was quite shocked - as my Spirit Guide had told me exactly how it would go. I was a little overwhelmed - and not for the first time in my life.

But just like all my other office jobs; I was struggling again, with the negativity that surrounded me. The 'vibe', alone, is enough to make me think of running far, far away. I have no control over my environment. The real problem for me is that once again I am starting to feel trapped and bored, unhappy in my endless days of office wear and repetitive tasks. My mind is beginning to wander, and my thoughts have turned to writing. It is as though my priorities are elsewhere and certainly, I feel as though my skills are not being used.

There is a lot simmering under the surface and a role in Admin just doesn't satisfy my wanderlust, in the office full time, 9-5 Monday to Friday, writing most evenings and weekends. Also being a mum to Dylan and wife to Rob means multi-tasking in an extreme sports kind of way!

So, there you have it, overall, my life is pretty standard and represents a lot of the same troubles any working mum would have.

I want you to be aware as you go on to read this book and I elaborate further on my relationship with my Spiritual Guide, Red Mountain, that I lead a pretty normal life. You will see that Red Mountain has been a constant in my life, coaching me and guiding me through different stages. You will see his words, which I have continued to record throughout my journey of development. When I listen and follow, things work out just as they should, and I feel fully supported, but when I stop listening and wander aimlessly, things can go very wrong.

Music has always played an important role in my life and I believe my parents weaned me on music. So, I have also included a playlist which goes hand-in-hand with the chapters – listen and 'tune in'.

I wasn't brought up in a community where Spirituality is a way of life. I wasn't christened with a wacky flower-power name. A *down-to-earth* Spirit Worker is who, and what, I am.

Love & Peace,

Nic.

FOUNDATION

Our experiences become the foundation of the future life we want to build.

To Begin...
Feeling Good – Nina Simone
ⓟ

Red Mountain...

"To begin is to start something as was intended. For the start brings about a sense of freshness. Freshness creates something within you that was intended to bring about something new for your soul to explore. There is a reason that you try different things and that reason is to deepen your knowledge. Think about all the information that you have gathered so far. It has not been worthless it is creating the person that you were supposed to be. This divert, and distraction has carried you through a period of time. It has served a purpose.

Nothing in your life has been for no reason. Everything has served and carried a valuable lesson. Each lesson, however tough and however deep only strengthens your soul and connection to the universe and how it unfolds around you.

You will never fully understand each lesson until you reach the other side, then when your journey and story is re-evaluated it will all become clear. Swallow these lessons and life's hardships with the knowing that they are not fruitless. It will all become so apparent - but not before the time is right for you.

You can handle all that is given to you. Have no doubts in your ability to cope with the lessons and hardship, you are more than equipped with a level of understanding that many do not possess. This will carry you through - never let the doubts and fears interrupt your inner knowledge.

You are loved eternally and even if the love you seek is not reciprocated, know that this is not a problem with your soul. It is the life's lessons of the other. You are a beautiful soul, too beautiful that you can incur damage from others. This damage will only allow you to have a deeper understanding of your journey.

This is a reminder that you are not responsible for the happiness of others. This is now a time for you to enjoy your own happiness. This is a period of time to be still and enjoy what is. No more moving forward, be still and enjoy your sweetness.

My Child... A time for you."

A Sagittarian Was Born

Everyone loves the Sunshine – Roy Ayres

A Sagittarian woman lacks tact and her flat, on-the-face statements may make you feel like running away from her. Then suddenly, she will say something so charming that you will feel as if you are on the seventh heaven. There you go again! You will be trapped in her charm once more. Once you have been enamoured by a Sagittarius, you will be staying with her for a long time.

She is pleasant, friendly, outspoken and very talkative. Her forthrightness comes from the fact that she has no illusions about the world. She sees it exactly as it is and says what she sees. At times, you may wish that she were not so honest. But then, she would be like any other girl, wouldn't she? In all probability, you will not like it.

A Sagittarian female is very optimistic, but she is not irrational. She will judge the entire situation as per the facts, analyse its probable outcome and still believe that things will get better. Usually, she is very calm and composed. However, when you become rude to her or offend her, she may become like the fire-spitting dragon. Sagittarius women are quite independent and love their freedom. They are attached to their family, but not too much.

With a Sagittarius girl, you will never have to guess. She says what she thinks and how she acts shows what she feels. This bluntness may cost her heavily at times, even to the point of ending relationships and situations. In any event, she would act as if she's not hurt at all and it is just one of the many harmless flirtations she's had. People will even believe all this, while inside she will be weeping and nursing her wounds. All this time, she will be analysing what went wrong and when.

The word 'marriage' makes a Sagittarian female a little nervous and you will need to tempt her in order to make her settle down. She is a little hard to catch and tends to be one of the boys at times. That doesn't mean she looks or acts like a man! In fact, she is as female as any other girl is.

The society and its norms do not matter to her. She can never be the hypocrite that some people are and tends to wiggle a few tongues.

Look deep inside a Sagittarius female and you will find a woman who is so enthusiastic about life and who trusts easily. In fact, this extreme belief makes her heart vulnerable and defenceless. It gets broken too often, but then, she knows how to move on with life quickly. You will be tempted to care for her. It's natural. There are hardly any people who can resist the bright and charming disposition of a Sagittarius girl.

She will not be too good with money and will most probably be on the extravagant side.

She is very sentimental and emotional, though it seems otherwise. It is just that, where her feelings are concerned, she becomes too shy.

A Sagittarian girl may pass the most sarcastic comments when she is angry, but she will forget the resentment soon enough. Then, she won't understand why you are so upset.

As a mother, she will be very friendly with the kids. In fact, she will be more of a chum, than a mum. Only, you must teach them to take her bluntness with a pinch of salt. Apart from that, she will be wonderful and make them as independent as she is.

Just let her be what she is. Don't try to change her and don't curb her individuality. She will brighten your life with her optimism, boost you with loyalty, trust you blindly and shower her affection on you. She will encourage you to see dreams and help you in making them come true!

-

So, there you have it, I feel this sums me up quite well. I am proud of my Sagittarius characteristics and I know that I can be blunt on occasion and a little too honest, but how can this be a fault? Surely everyone wants to hear the truth, right? I find it hard to operate in any other way.

I also note that it says we move on quickly and I am so grateful to have this trait, as it has carried me through life. Life certainly has had its ups and downs but if I hadn't been so adaptable, I could have given myself the 'Victim Crown'. We all have troubles in our life and didn't Buddha say that 'life is full of struggles'?

1976

Isn't she Lovely – Stevie Wonder

ⓘ

I'm told the summer of 1976 was a scorcher. The 1976 heatwave led to the hottest Summer average in the UK since records began. It was one of the driest, sunniest and warmest summers.

This was the summer that my mum carried me. This was the year that a nation of mothers-to-be wore smock tops and ridiculously large sunglasses and long hair with centre partings. The fashion of the 70's was something special. This was the decade of bell-bottoms, outrageously large wide-open collars, with a little flash of a hairy chest. Not forgetting the platform shoes with 5 or 6-inch heels! I've seen the old sepia Polaroid's and I'd say they were pretty shocking.

I was the first and only child to my parents and the first of the Grandchildren to be born, the first Niece and one of the first babies in my parent's friendship group.

I, Nicola Louise Debley, was born on 26th November 1976, a Sagittarian. I was a good healthy weight, with a "nice" yellow jaundice tint to my skin tone. I was happy and healthy.

My parents were still very young when I was born; my mum was 21 and my Dad a few years older. They married on my Mum's eighteenth birthday. Crazy young! At eighteen, I had not yet even fallen in love or had a "proper" relationship, let alone been of sound mind to consider marriage.

As a family we started off in a house in Union Street Dunstable. It was a small Victorian terrace. My mum became friendly with the lady over the road, who'd had daughter three months after I was born. Emma Louise and I were to become lifelong friends. I have always considered Emma to be like my sister. We have been through many experiences together and have drifted in and out of each other's lives continually.

Now in our forties we are tighter than ever and seem to have a timeless bond and a shared understanding that seals our friendship even further. I love Emma dearly and I am grateful for her continued support and loyalty. It's not often you have a friendship from birth, and a friendship like ours is to be truly cherished.

As expected at such a young age, I do not remember too much about this house or the time that we spent there. From photos, I have seen a few grainy images of seventies birthday parties; dark images of our best long frilly, party dresses, homemade *Magic Roundabout* cakes and plenty of jelly and ice cream. There was no expense spared with the coloured paper- chain decorations and I'm sure a few games of sleeping lions and musical chairs had been played. 'Sleeping Lions' was always the adults' favourite game and now I understand why!

We moved to Victoria Street when I was around two, it was another Victorian Terrace. Long before Location, Location, Location and other such property programs, my parents were knocking down walls, tearing out kitchens and bathrooms and generally renovating properties. Painting the walls, a shade of Magnolia and tempting potential buyers with the prospect of owning a new home with their very own Avocado Bathroom suite, then selling up and moving on.

The time at Victoria Street was when I started to recall some very distant memories. I remember our house was always a busy home, with plenty of people, lots of laughter, loud music and big characters. My parents had plenty of parties, with a Jukebox playing, which would shape my taste in music for years to come; from Led Zeppelin's Stairway to Heaven to The Police and then Pink Floyd to The Rolling Stones.

I was always hanging out with grownups. I guess from a young age, I was always an observer and from what I understand, I was quite quiet and well behaved. I learnt very quickly that was the best way to be, if I wanted to hang out with the grownups, I had to 'blend in', to go un-noticed, slip under the radar, and so I did.

Genuine

We Will Rock You – Queen

ⓓ

It was in Victoria Street that my 'friend' Genuine appeared. I was an only child with an imaginary friend, nothing unusual there, although as I have gotten older, I have since connected my Spirituality to this phase in my life. Maybe it wasn't such a coincidence? To be honest, I do not remember much about Genuine, although my Mum and Dad have both reminded me of her.

My memory is not clear, but I am told that I had met my 'friend' around the age of 2. This friend was with me all the time and I would chew things over with her or talk to her about my Mum and Dad if they had told me off and sit next to her at the table and eat dinner. You get the idea, general friendship stuff between a two-year-old and her best friend.

No one else could see her, only me. She was special. I do not remember this friendship or have any recollection of it, but as I sit here now, writing retrospectively, it would seem like a clear indication that I may have had a little link to the Spirit world right from the word go.

From what I understand, it is quite common for kids to have an imaginary friend.

Eileen Kennedy-Moore, PhD writing for Psychology Today gives the stats that around 37% of children will have an imaginary friend by the time they are seven. Eileen also suggests that, "It seems logical that children who invent invisible friends might be lonely or have social problems, but research doesn't support those assumptions. In fact, compared to those who don't create them, children with imaginary companions (either invisible friends or personified objects) tend to be less shy, engage in more laughing and smiling with peers, and do better at tasks involving imagining how someone else might think."

-

I cannot say for sure that my friendship with Genuine, was a sign of connecting to Spirit; it doesn't confirm any Spiritual gift however it does show a creative and imaginative child.

West Street, My Happy House
Blue Monday - New Order
ⓘ

We moved from Victoria Street again to a new house, ripe for renovation. But this time, West Street was the *Location, Location, Location*.

This house was awesome in my eyes. It had plenty of space to play and the garden was a good size with a playing field at the back of us. One day in particular stands out, I was walking our dog, Paddy, on a lead in the back garden. God knows how, but all of a sudden, he took a leap onto the garden wall and dive bombed his little fury arse into the playing field below.

Now, my Mum had made me promise not to let go of him whatever I did, so as promised, I held onto him tight! The only problem was there was a drop between our garden wall and the grass of the playing field below. My poor little dog was just a little short of landing safely as I held on tight to the lead. Scraping and grazing my arms as I held on tight for what seemed like an eternity. Thankfully, a mad dash from a grown- up, who had the superhuman ability to have eyes in the back of their head, saved mine and poor Paddy's life.

Not only did we have a large drop for a suicidal dog in our garden, we also had a brick-built barbeque which was the best pretend Fish and Chip Shop ever. I used to play happily for hours with my friends, wrapping 'fish and chips' in newspaper.

In the bathroom, we had a very on-trend brown suite which also consisted of its very own 'elevator'!

It may have looked like a shower to anyone else but to me it would take me to the top of the world and back.

I have so many good memories from this house. It was my happy house.

With my curly hair and freckles, I had always felt scruffy. Imagine a Brunette version of 'Annie', this was how I felt. I had a friend who had beautiful shiny black straight glowing hair. She was always immaculately dressed in 'Daz'-white pinafores and shiny patent shoes. Then there was me with dungarees and a crazy Afro. It didn't help matters that I think my Dad thought I was a boy…

One example of this was when I was woken up in the middle of the night to a tiny red kid's motocross bike in the hall way. Slightly dangerous, as I did go on to run Dad over whilst riding it one day.

Living in my happy house I started to be aware of 'the voices'. Oh dear, that sounds very crazy doesn't it? How else can I put it? I was a kid and it was a very unusual experience.

I was aware that I could hear multiple conversations from many different people all at once, but I was unable to see these people. It would always happen when I was playing alone in my bedroom. Spirit would always come forward, when I was at my most relaxed and receptive. I would hear many people talking and it would be so very annoying. Imagine eavesdropping on a telephone exchange, where several conversations are all happening at once. It was difficult to make sense of what was being said and I found it very hard to deal with.

My head would sometimes feel a little strange; it was like I was receiving a radio transmission. The voices I heard sounded excited and happy and wanted to keep talking. Some of them would just be chatting amongst themselves. It seemed they may have had an urgent message, but I was unable to decipher it.

However, confusing it was I never felt afraid of the 'Spirit chatter'. It always felt as though I was being looked after, watched and cared for.

Looking back, it was at this stage in my life that my journey began. This was the turning point for me – I was now at the very beginning of this long and enriching path, working for Spirit. Whether I chose to follow or not at any given time, my path was there, all mapped out and ready for me.

Even though West Street was the time that I became aware of my connection to Spirit, my Mum has since told me that it was actually in Victoria Street, that I made her aware that I was hearing Spirit. She told me of a time when I came galloping down the stairs to her and my Dad to tell them that I kept hearing voices and explaining that I had asked them to slow down because I was getting confused.

My Mum has said that she would tell me to ask them to slow down or ask them to go away. She would ask me if I knew what they were saying, but I didn't. I think that is what was so frustrating for me; too many people were talking at once, it was like being in a busy pub, where you can't hear yourself think. If I had of been able to make more sense of it, I believe I would have found it all a bit easier.

From what I have learnt from my Mum, I started to hear voices around the same time as I became BFF with Genuine.

I think it is something that many people experience as a child, but for fear of ridicule, they choose not to mention it. Like me, many children were unsure of how to process the connection they had, unable to understand exactly what was happening. Some parents may have dismissed such claims from their 'crazy' children I guess it would be pretty spooky for some grown-ups if your child came to tell you that they "see or hear dead people!"

It's a tough one to deal with as a parent. Thank goodness my Mum and Dad were, and still are, very open-minded. It was easy enough to share this with my mum. My Dad was neither believing nor disbelieving. He was just accepting and open to what I was saying. Neither my Mum nor Dad ever made me feel like I was totally bonkers. Thank god, I must have chosen the right parents! However, I didn't tell anyone else. I knew this was not a normal situation. It was not for sharing and I knew that it was something quite unique and special.

-

As a parent you can always teach your child to ask the Spirit to step back and give instructions to Spirit to "Go Away", just as my Mum did. If a child does become frightened at any time, Spirit should always respect this and, as a parent you can also ask them to step back. I actually didn't become scared at all. I am told that initially I was puzzled by what was happening, and then had a period of acceptance. But by the time I moved to West Street, and I have more of a memory of it, I know that I was becoming angry.

Mum tells me that I would get quite cross and say, "It's no good trying to speak to me, all at once, I can't understand you!"

In fact, I used to get so angry, that I would hit out, hoping to stop the chatter.

Many children will see or hear Spirit. They are far more intuitive and have not reached a point in their life where they begin to shut out intuition, through sensible and rational thinking.

'Connecting to Spirit' could be described as quite a primitive, naturally inherited, behaviour and our intuition is designed to keep us safe. They are very open to connecting with their guides and lost loved ones. Equally, Spirit are overjoyed when they are able to find a connection. A child, who can connect at such a young age, is highly likely to go on to use their gift in adulthood, unless they prefer not to, in which case it will lay dormant until developed further.

-

The truth is we all have the ability to communicate with Spirit if we choose to use it. The sad thing is that many people are not aware, they hide or bury their gift, perhaps out of scepticism or doubt in their ability or because they lack the dedication to learning and developing their gift further.

When a child connects to Spirit, commonly, this is a relative or someone the child is familiar with. For example, the child may tell you that they have seen or spoken with Grandad after he 'died'. Understandably, this can be upsetting to the family. However, in my case, I later learned that I was connecting with the higher realms of the Spirit world and with my Guides using 'Clairaudience'. This means clear hearing and is the power to hear sound from the Spirit world.

As a child, I found this stage in my life quite alarming and I am grateful to my Mum, as she was always open and would let me talk to her about the chatter I was hearing. I always knew that it was very important for me not to discuss this with anyone. I knew I was different and that was ok but I didn't want people to think I was bonkers.

It certainly is a tough subject, even to this day. Many years ago, anyone who heard voices was considered to be possessed, insane, or mentally disturbed. They would have been locked away in straight-jackets or executed, as was the case for Joan of Arc. There are many Gurus and Wise Men, who have recorded the voices they heard, in which they were given teachings, wisdom and guidance.

Reassuringly, the mental health charity Mind, explains that some people hear a voice as part of a Spiritual experience.* This may be a very special experience and one that you feel helps you make sense of your life.

https://www.mind.org.uk/information-support/types-of-mental-health-problems/hearing-voices

-

As a child I was scared; scared of the dark, scared of my toys, scared of the curtains being open at night time.

There was one night that is forever etched in my memory. This dark night, I remember waking up to see a man climbing up the glass of my window, he wasn't a normal man, he was dressed in black but had a mask on that made him look like a cat. I called him cat man. My Mum tells me that I went running into my parents' room in the middle of the night telling horrors of seeing a man climbing up my window. Dad went to look but found nothing unusual.

Mum remembers that I asked to speak to her more about it in the morning. She told me that I wasn't the sort of child to make up stories and I wasn't one to create things just for attention. Therefore, she knew that this had to be something very major. My Mum believes that I really saw something that night, simply because of my reaction.

I remember clearly that the 'Cat Man' had looked at me, as though this 'crazy afro-haired' kid had somehow disturbed *him*! He stopped for a moment and looked back at me, before he continued his climb up the glass of my window. I was so passionate as I relived everything and told my Mum, "I wasn't dreaming!"

It was after this event, that I made a pact with Spirit, that I was never to see anything as I was so afraid of what I might see.

This fear continued well into my teens. I have been reassured by many mediums that Spirit were aware of me being scared and confirmed the pact that I had made as a small child of about 6; I never wanted to 'see' any Spirits, or anything that would scare me ever again.

I remember a message I received from a local Medium. My Nanny Eva came through, telling me to not be afraid of a TV Program, called *Most Haunted*. I used to watch it, but only in the day time and I would hold my breath whilst watching it. Nanny Eva's message told me to, "stop watching that bloody programme" and to not believe all that was being shown. Thanks Nan, that really did help me a lot.

My friend and honorary sister, Lisa still mocks me now for being such a scaredy-cat; how can a medium be scared of ghosts?

When we were much younger, Lisa would be watching *A Nightmare on Elm Street* and I would be playing in the kitchen, so I didn't have to watch it. I still lovingly refer to her now as Wednesday Addams (and I'm the one who talks to Spirit!)

At this age, I took a trip with Mum and Dad. It was quite a journey and partly responsible for planting the travel-bug seeds within me. We took a train journey through Europe, travelling through Italy and Switzerland. We would pass many snow-covered mountains, alpine meadows and lakes. It was so exciting!

We would jump off at a new station in a new country; pick up some freshly baked bread and coffees and juice for me! I loved travelling, and this was something we did quite a lot; having plenty of holidays and adventures. I was happy to be ambling around old ruins and historic towns in Europe; smelling and tasting different foods, flavours and cultures.

-

As with all our houses, it soon became boring, and a new challenge was on the horizon. We packed the tea chests again and off we went to Somerset. I don't remember communicating with Spirit after West Street. I think it came to an abrupt stop when we moved into the Pub, time became frozen.

The Pub

Don't You Want Me – Human League

Things began to change and unravel. My happy little world started to unfold. I was seven when we moved to Highbridge in Somerset. A rundown Hotel & Pub was the next challenge for my still young parents, mine was a new school. We moved with my Dad's father, my Grandad but I never saw him as a Grandad; he was just this cold, aloof, very tall grey-haired guy. I don't think we ever even had a conversation.

I can't say I ever felt totally part of this new school. I always felt like a bit of an outsider, like a square peg in a round hole. With my cockney accent and big frizzy hairdo, I did stand out quite a bit. Thankfully though, I made a very good friend. She was small, petite, and very cute; I remember her dimples when she smiled. We bonded quickly, and I am so grateful for her help in making the 'Londoner' fit in with the West Country kids. She would come over to play in the Pub and we would create games and we invented our own imaginary worlds, losing ourselves in the maze of corridors and rooms within the pub. Thanks to Facebook we are still in contact now.

My parents were running a pub, and I was free to explore; plenty of Britvic Pineapple for me and freedom, as I would roam around the skittle alley, hotel and function room. There was a drum kit in there that I was able to use to try and make something sound like music, but really it was more like noise.

One time, I remember riding around the car park on a Racer bike. All was going well, until I flipped off to the side and crash-landed into the local hairdresser's yellow Vauxhall Nova, smashing his headlight and costing my Dad more than a few ciders on the House!

The pub/hotel/café was huge, and I spent a lot of time hanging out with Lady. Lady was our beautiful German Shephard. I had a very strong connection and bond with Lady. I loved her; she was a very special dog. She passed away when I was 15 and I really struggled, as she had always felt like some kind of sister. Yes, I know it's odd and I can assure you, I was no wolf child, but we had a very strong bond. I was able to look into her eyes and sense what she was thinking, and I'm pretty sure she understood my emotions too. It wasn't just me that loved Lady, we all loved Lady.

I had my eighth birthday party in the pub and I was allowed to invite everyone from my class; even the horrible girl, who was obviously not very keen on me. It was a great disco and I loved it - the last big high, before the big low.

D.I.V.O.R.C.E

Moneys Too Tight - Simply Red
▷

We returned to Dunstable. I returned to my previous school Icknield Lower School and we lived in a rental for a short period of time, and then once again back to a doer upper in Princess Street; as had always been done before.

Only this time the doer upper didn't get done up. My mum and Dad split. Dad had an affair, with our next-door neighbour and while he certainly had his own, very valid and genuine reasons, it all could have been handled better. But as I understand more with age, it's clear that things were very difficult.

My Dad had known something quite awful about my Mum's childhood and what she had experienced at the hands of her narcissistic, psychopathic Father. My Mum, not knowing any better, wanted my Dad to keep this a secret so as not to have any impact on the rest of the family. It was quite a huge and dreadfully difficult situation to handle, for both of them. Would anyone know the right way to overcome this sort of dilemma? Whilst trying to keep an essence of normality…

This stage of my life hurt like hell.

The harmony that I had once known had now become total and utter chaos. It seemed my Dad was the bad guy and my Mum was the victim.

Visiting my Dad and his new family was extremely hard for me; I didn't feel like I belonged at all. My new family now consisted of a step-mum, stepbrother and stepsister.

Amazingly, I had always longed for a brother or sister and yet when they arrived, it wasn't how I imagined it to be. They say you have to be careful what you wish for. Once more I regressed, feeling like the scruffy little kid.

On one hand I felt I'd lost my Dad but on the other, I also gained a brother and sister. It wasn't like true siblings though, it was more like a 'them and me' situation. I watched on as they stole my father's attention and priorities. I watched on as I felt their life was easier than mine, as life began to get harder and harder. I watched on as I felt they were spoilt and presented with opportunities to better their future.

I remember my step-sister's birthday... We all went up to the stables, where we used to take weekly riding lessons. There we waited, as my sister was presented with a beautiful white pony with a big red ribbon; her birthday surprise.

I guess I should have been happy for her, but I wasn't. I felt like I wanted to burst into tears and run away. It was so hard to hold the tears at bay. Again, I was just so flipping sad. One day, I promised myself, I will have that horse. A horse of my very own, to take care of, that will make everything better!

-

My Mum dealt with a lot of hurt and, as a sensitive child, I probably felt and absorbed most of these emotions. There was no shelter from the pain that my Mum was experiencing. Not only had she lost her husband, she also had to deal with the facts. My Dad couldn't cope with knowing the truth and could not stand to be in the same room with his Father-in-law. How did my Mum cope with the fact that the abuse she suffered as a child, not only ruined her self-esteem, confidence and life, it also ruined her marriage and her child's security?

Yes, there were other reasons that led to the end of their marriage but indirectly the abuse that my Mum suffered affected how she lived, and her relationships.

At that time, living with Mum was about endurance. Times were hard. Both Mum and Dad lost so much money on the pub. Now Mum was left alone to pay the bills and the mortgage on this imposing house. She took in lodgers and I had to grow up quickly. Speaking to my Mum's good friend and lodger at the time, I have since learnt even more about the sheer poverty of those times. For a day out, we would go to a forest near us called Ashridge. A great place to go for a family day out! Only it was a totally different agenda for us. We were there to fill up the boot of Mum's Vauxhall Nova with wood for the open fires at home. This wood would heat the whole house, but it wasn't the only fuel for the fire I was told. Mum's friend would also kindly help my Mum, with her financial worries and feed the hungry flames with the never-ending supply of bills and debts that came through the door, courtesy of Royal Mail. She would say, "If you can't pay them, let's burn them."

During this time, my Mum made some very crazy dinners; some good and some not so good. She was creative, and it was a good job because she had to be! A regular weekly food shop was just not an option in our house.

I remember being embarrassed by my packed lunches at school, hiding my lunches under the desks at lunchtime. I never knew what little surprises would be in there for me, all I wanted was a cheese sandwich and crisps like my friends. I would end up with some left overs and other snacks - not very kid-friendly.

When a girl loses her stability at 9 years old and her world is turned upside down, the knock-on effect is tremendous. I had a huge gaping hole in my heart. With Dad leaving there was a lack of stability. I could have coped better but that just couldn't be the case with my Mum's parents sharking around, encouraging negative emotions.

It says that independence is a characteristic of a Sagittarius and I learnt that very quickly. Mum was working hard, and I was walking home from school at 10, home alone and doing the washing and drying up every day.

The more I learn and the older I have become, the more I understand the decisions that were made by my parents. It is all too easy to allow the actions of the past to make up your judgments. We all make mistakes and I will never judge my parents on this very difficult stage of their lives.

Thankfully during this tough time in my life, I met my beautiful friend, Lisa. We were thrown together by the same friend and lodger. Lisa was also from a single parent family and an only child, like me. On our first meeting, I was so emotional that all I did was cry. That day I must have been so bewildered by all that had happened and what was still happening, that I just needed to ball. And I did, in Lisa's face. Snotty and teary, we bonded instantly.

We have always had such a great understanding of each other's journey and an even deeper understanding of each other's childhood. She knows me inside out and we still have each other's back through thick and thin. Soul Sisters. Neither of us have had a traditional upbringing and sometimes this may have made us appear different, but it was these differences that brought us closer together.

It is not all one sided though, as I certainly helped Lisa too. Without my intervention, she was certainly heading for trouble at school with her *geek-chic* look. I could not let this happen to my lovely friend and tucked her under my wing.

Lisa has said, "Nic has always been different to my other friends. She has always demonstrated great strength in her own mind.

Even when we were younger, Nic used to guide me, not always for the good, as she would sometimes possibly lead me astray. But she has always been a leader rather than a follower. Nic, knows me and I like to think I know Nic. We read each other well. Although Nic is Spiritual and this was evident in her outlook on life, I didn't even witness this as we were growing up. Nothing that would have brought me to the attention of her skills, which she has honed now.

Nic and I are opposite, like day and night, but even though we are opposite we meet in the middle and complement each other's persona.

My only criticism of Nic is that she is to remain focussed and follow what's in her heart, as her heart always seems to know what is best."

Chaotic Lifestyle and Addiction
Fast Car – Tracy Chapman
ⓘ

Red Mountain…

"Times have evolved; new life brings many challenges and questions. Your life has not been easy My Child; it is no wonder at times you feel torment and trouble. Many of the people around you do not know exactly, what you have experienced and felt. Your sensitivity has given you a different experience and perception to those that have walked the very same path as you.

The lava that runs through your blood stream has absorbed so much hurt, anger and terror from those around you. Your parents bear the scars from parents unable to parent or care, as any decent parent should.

Your parents may not have given you all that you needed, but they gave you all that they could with the circumstances they were raised in.

A time of torture for both and fragmented lines of trust, gave grounds for an unusual start for you. You were never to be just an average child. Your emotions run deeper, similar to the lines engraved into a fallen birch. Many, many layers."

My life as a child, from what I remember, was always chaotic. I didn't have the routines that many of my friends had. I would mock my friends that went swimming on a Monday, or ballet every Wednesday or had regular hobbies and interests. I thought these routines and familiarity were only for the boring, predictable people; when truthfully, I desperately wanted a piece of their normal pie.

In my house, as a child, there wasn't a lot of peace and calm. After my Dad left the house it was full of chaos, parties, stress and unrest. This was my normal. If it wasn't the arguments between my Mum and Stepdad, and there were plenty of those, there would be a drama created by my Mum's parents. To gain respite from this stress, they would throw a good party, lots of music and plenty of drinking. These parties were always fun, and I absolutely loved them.

The reason for this utter madness is because my Mum and Stepdad were both addicts. They both had their own addictions which helped them to cope with their hidden pain. My Mum's world and chaotic lifestyle was due to the after effects of abuse.

My Mum wasn't a drunk nor a druggie, she had an underlying addiction and this often affected her priorities.

I believe to some degree, we are all trying to be better than our parents. Many of us will blame our parents for the 'issues' we have. We are all trying to overcome some failures and shortfalls and for my Mum that isn't too hard as her parents were simply diabolical.

My Mum far excelled her parents' nurturing skills. I always felt loved and cherished.

I am aware that I may overcompensate with my son, Dylan and be too conscientious, trying not to damage him in anyway. It may even be the case that I over-parent him for fear of under-parenting.

I always feel the need to have control over anything and everything around me, I seek perfectionism, and I am my own worst critic - this may be as a result of a negative internal dialogue and lack of confidence, and I can be very sensitive to criticism from others. I also have a very deeply-seated fear of rejection; I had taken my Dad's departure personally and completely felt as though he was trying to escape from me as well as my Mum. Therefore, if my Dad could reject me, so could someone else, anyone else, including future relationships.

Before I began a relationship, I needed to feel secure.

I always knew that my Mum loved me. She has given me lots of reassurance and encouragement throughout my life. And my self-esteem, although I'm sure it could be better, has never been low. My Mum installed a great sense of worth in me and she ensured that she made up her losses in me.

Red Mountain…

"You were not taught many of the life lessons you needed, and you were partly left to raise yourself and choose your own path.

There is resentment within you that you did not receive the calm that you wanted. Your mother had many issues, and unfortunately, you suffered as a consequence. Your father loved but was unable to show it completely.

A child so lost – only you could find your way in this jungle, that is your life. You are still learning your way, but soon you will be free.

For as you approach the next chapter, your childhood is replaced, and a woman you have become. Rising from the shadows, emerging with strength and building new paternal relationships.

You have no choice, other than that, of courage, to shape your own future. Take guidance from Spirit, with nothing but love – your next chapter brings freedom."

EXPLORATION

We are eager to learn new things and begin to explore the world outside our family.

Life as a Teenager

No Woman, No Cry – Bob Marley

As my Mum was keen to promote independence and an understanding of money, I started to work from a young age. I remember I was finishing school at 3.30pm then walking into town to get a bus to the North end of Dunstable, then walking to the other end of town to my Uncle and Auntie's house and I would spend the next couple of hours looking after my cousins.

I'm not sure how long I did this. As much as I loved and still do love them enormously, I'm not sure this is what I wanted to be doing every day after school. However, I was earning money from a young age and I was enjoying the financial freedom it gave me. I think this job allowed me to save for my Disco Roller Skates. They were white leather with bright pink wheels - classy!

My next job was as a Stable Hand. I loved this job with my whole heart! Every Saturday I would go up to the yard and muck out the horses then tack them up ready for the lessons. I would prepare the feeds and turn them out into the fields. What I also really enjoyed, was working with the RDA (Riding for the Disabled Association) children. I would walk with them and lead their horses as they enjoyed the therapy of the horses and lessons. This was a huge part of my love for horses when I was younger. I used to enjoy riding and competing in a few competitions at weekends.

After the Yard, I started working in a Bakery. I would go to the Bakery around the corner from me in Dunstable. Two mornings a week before school; I started work at 7am. It was my responsibility to put out the freshly baked bread, pies and pasties. I'd have to jam and sugar the doughnuts, ice the buns and serve customers. I would also work two evenings after school and every other Saturday. I would get paid the whopping sum of £7.50 per week!

I skipped through my middle school, hanging out with my very bestest friend. Emma and I were very, very different; Emma was very intelligent and studious, studying for her music grades, either in piano or clarinet. I, on the other hand, was arty and a little bit more haphazard than Emma. Although, I did want to play the clarinet to be more like her. Unfortunately, I ended up with the spare clarinet from school. It was too embarrassing to carry the old beaten up box it came in, so the risk of losing credibility won and I ditched the lessons for fear of ridicule.

Emma and I spent many days roller-skating around her Close and when Emma got a paper round, I used to help her. I think we may have morphed into each other at some stage; wearing the same coloured Desert Boots, hooded top and Aladdin pants. We turned up to a 13th birthday party once, looking like twins and we even had the same haircuts.

When Emma and I spent time together we laughed constantly; the kind of laughter that made our bellies and jaws ache. It's contagious; once one of us starts we are doomed, even now.

I asked Emma if she had any thoughts on the work that I do now and how I connect to Spirit. She said to me, "It's hard as I don't see you being any different, you are just Nikki to me!"

This sounds about right as we are just comfortable and unaware of anything. It's as it has always been, and nothing will change us; we've been the same for forty years. We have been walking this life together.

At 13, I went to Northfields Upper School. This was when I began to change massively. No longer was I the quiet and good Nicola. Now I was a teenager and I had crazy hormones and curiosity hijacking my thought process.

These crazy hormones lead me down a very wonky path. My other friend Emma J and I started to experiment. These experiments included taking Acid at the weekends. We were 15; this was far too young. Emma very sensibly *(not)* documented these crazy weekends in her diary, which her Mum found and read...

I remember the day so clearly; when my Mum told me she had been called to the school to meet with the Deputy Head (who was also a former teacher to my Mum). My Mum was informed that I was using Acid and she exploded on me when she got home. Goodness gracious me! How long was I grounded for on that occasion? I'm pretty sure I didn't see daylight for a very long time!

Emma and I are still the closest of friends. Emma lives in Egypt with her husband and 3 of her 4 children. We keep in touch all the time. Only now, our conversations are much different. Emma is now following Islam and she is the most content I have ever known her. We both follow our Spiritual paths and have great respect and understanding for each other's journey. Maybe we were both looking for something more in our crazy teenage years?

Understandably, my grades began to suffer due to my 'soul-searching habits'. I was no longer a good student. Intelligent yes, I am told, but I was unwilling to apply myself. I was bored in class as the lessons did not inspire me, nor did I see the need to take part and fully engage; unless of course it was Art or PE or occasionally English when something really caught my attention. As a child, I was never a troublemaker or disruptive. I just did my own thing quietly and opted out.

I wonder now if this was due to me picking up some unsavoury recreational habits that did nothing, other than quash my motivation and zest for life?

I was smoking far too much weed.

Hmmm… not very good at all and I am very ashamed of this now but on the flip side, this did catapult my creativity. I was creating some beautiful silk screen prints and psychedelic artwork and so I was gaining very good grades in Art. Music and Art were becoming my staple diet. Art at college was the next obvious choice, until I gave up. Again, weed was having a very negative effect on my commitment and enthusiasm for life.

Back then I was listening to music from Bob Marley, Led Zeppelin, Pink Floyd, The Rolling Stones and other music of the 90's like Blur and Oasis.

I loved Art and being creative, but I still felt slightly torn. I also liked working with people and did consider Healthcare as an option but how was I to combine creativity and helping people? I didn't have the answers as a teenager. I was still trying to figure things out.

~

As a teenager I would often go to the SNU (Spiritualist National Union) church with my Mum. It was held above a pub one evening in the week in the Star & Garter, Dunstable.

I can remember the strong smell and thick fog of cigarette smoke. No smoking ban in those days and this was not your normal Church; it was very different. It was a Church for Healers and Mediums and we would go along to receive messages and get healing.

Mum said that I had asked her to go when I was around 14. On one hand, I was leading a crazy hedonistic teenage lifestyle and on the other hand, I was mingling with mediums and healers; the balance of life - just like Yin and Yang.

I am told that I was very accepting of the idea that there was an Afterlife, as though it was a given. Mum said I was never afraid or frightened.

At this young age, I was having readings from platform mediums, telling me that I would develop a deeper connection and communicate with Spirit. I would be told that it was my destiny to work for Spirit. I would ponder on it for a couple of days and then discuss it a little further with Mum at a pace that was right for me.

At around 16, immediately after some very forgettable GCSE exams, me and my friends drove down to Somerset in a 'Noddy car'. We jumped in the car, a beautiful burgundy and yellow Morris Minor and blasted 'Get Off Of My Cloud' as we drove down the M4 and M5; breaking down a few times along the way...

With a very large bag of green, some Acid and a whole big bag of freedom; my kaftan was packed, my feet were in sandals and I was living the dream.

We met up with some other friends and pitched up our tents. I had died and gone to heaven! I had my sandals on and the sun was shining. Back then, it didn't seem to rain like it does now during the festival season. There was no need to pack wellies in those days!

To me, this felt like I was in my Spiritual home. My once ridiculous Afro that I'd had when I was a kid was now okay. I had finally learned to love and accept my unique hairdo. It suited my image. I was Hippy Nic and still am according to my very good friends, The Kavanaghs!

The year was 1993, I was at Glastonbury and the acts included The Orb, Lenny Kravitz, Velvet Underground, Galliano and Stereo MCs. It's a good job I was able to Google this information as unfortunately I am unable to remember anyone that I saw that weekend; I was too busy skipping around in a kaftan on Acid, thinking I was at Woodstock! I was also a little blind as I didn't like to wear my glasses so was also very short-sighted.

These days I am more likely to be at a festival with my son Dylan and my Mum or Dad, and a smaller low-key festival. So, things are a little different!

Raving
DJ Randall

In the late 90's when I was in my mid to late teens I was spending most of my time writing, listening to music and still smoking too much weed. 'Acid House' and raving was all the rage, so I was partying hard at the weekend in unused warehouses.

Late at night we would jump in someone's car and join a very long queue of cars on a convoy. This convoy would traipse and snake around Luton and Dunstable town through Business Parks and Petrol Stations. This would go on for many hours, until someone would be given 'the nod' and we would head off to a derelict warehouse or field, weather depending.

I remember one night, jumping through an open window of a disused warehouse and being helped by many random ravers and organisers. Still now, I can feel the weight of my humiliation crushing me as I landed flat on my arse. Not very 'cool'.

We were all one big group of ravers, dancing all night to some jungle beats or Drum 'n' Bass. Feeling the love and the bassline vibrating through your body. All was good while you were up but inevitably, what goes up must come down. By 9.00am in the morning the expressions on people's faces were not pretty. Everyone, except for the odd Raver who was still going strong, was trying to get home; bundling into Ford Escorts or Vauxhall

Cavaliers. Reality had come to bite us on the bum and it was time to go home and deal with a very nasty comedown.

The weekends were about partying and staying awake until the birds started to sing. The weekdays were about finding myself once more, after the weekend had robbed me of my soul. Usually by about Wednesday, I'd be back to normal, ready to start the weekend again on a Thursday night.

I don't know how I managed to go to work on a Friday after clubbing the night before!

Nanny Eva

You'll Never Walk Alone – Gerry & The Pacemakers

My lovely Nanny Eva passed away on my 18th Birthday. I loved my Nanny Eva. She was my storyteller and my cake maker. All those lovely homely things. She would curse me for my hair and wear a scarf around hers, as we walked to the shops. She would *'eff and jeff'* as we watched *Big Daddy* and *Giant Haystacks* wrestling on TV.

She was a proper Londoner, born in Highbury, North London, right near the Arsenal football ground. Nan would tell me stories of nights spent in the underground hiding from those "bleeding German Bombers". She would tell me stories from the war. Telling me how her children would go to school in the morning after a night of bombing; only to discover their little friends had not survived the night before.

She would tell me stories of singsongs "Knees up, Mother Brown" around the piano and how she watched her Uncles marching down the street as they returned home from war.

I would spend the Summer holidays with my Nan at her house. It was familiar, and I will never forget the taste of her coconut cakes, they were legendary!

Nanny Eva still guides me now, with her humour and support.

Words of Wisdom
Us & Them – Pink Floyd

During my time at college and raving years, I did a stint of stacking shelves in Wilko's. Then I worked as a call handler for a TV rental company which then turned into full time job when I dropped out of college. I worked my way up to the glittering heights of Team Leader.

During these years I also began to spend a lot of time in quiet reflection, writing and collecting pieces of writing that inspired me. I had journals filled with quotes and inspirational writing. I didn't realise at the time, but I knew these words just flowed and it felt like I was being guided to write certain pieces of wisdom. I knew this was a significant time in my life and I felt very connected to my own soul and its journey.

Some of the pieces that particularly inspired me at the time were The Desiderata, The Serenity Prayer and Footprints. Even as a party-loving teenager, I was searching for something different. I knew there was more to life. The beauty of the words and the use of language inspired me.

Desiderata…

Go placidly amid the noise and haste,
and remember what peace there may be in silence.
As far as possible without surrender
be on good terms with all persons.
Speak your truth quietly and clearly;
and listen to others,
even the dull and the ignorant;
they too have their story.

Avoid loud and aggressive persons,
they are vexations to the Spirit.
If you compare yourself with others,
you may become vain and bitter;
for always there will be greater and lesser persons than yourself.
Enjoy your achievements as well as your plans.

Keep interested in your own career, however humble;
it is a real possession in the changing fortunes of time.
Exercise caution in your business affairs;
for the world is full of trickery.
But let this not blind you to what virtue there is;
many persons strive for high ideals;
and everywhere life is full of heroism.

Be yourself.
Especially, do not feign affection.
Neither be cynical about love;
for in the face of all aridity and disenchantment
it is as perennial as the grass.

EXPLORATION

Take kindly the counsel of the years,
gracefully surrendering the things of youth.
Nurture strength of Spirit to shield you in sudden misfortune.

But do not distress yourself with dark imaginings.
Many fears are born of fatigue and loneliness.
Beyond a wholesome discipline,
be gentle with yourself.

You are a child of the universe,
no less than the trees and the stars;
you have a right to be here.
And whether or not it is clear to you,
no doubt the universe is unfolding as it should.

Therefore, be at peace with God,
whatever you conceive Him to be,
and whatever your labours and aspirations,
in the noisy confusion of life keep peace with your soul.

With all its sham, drudgery, and broken dreams,
it is still a beautiful world.
Be cheerful.
Strive to be happy.

-Max Ehrmann, 1926, Desiderata

God grant me the serenity
to accept the things I cannot change;
courage to change the things I can;
and wisdom to know the difference.

Living one day at a time;
enjoying one moment at a time;
accepting hardships as the pathway to peace;
taking, as He did, this sinful world
as it is, not as I would have it;
trusting that He will make all things right
if I surrender to His Will;
that I may be reasonably happy in this life
and supremely happy with Him
forever in the next.
Amen.

-Reinhold Niebuhr (1892-1971), Serenity Prayer

The Footprints Prayer

One night I had a dream...

I dreamed I was walking along the beach with the Lord, and across the sky flashed scenes from my life. For each scene, I noticed two sets of footprints in the sand; one belonged to me, and the other to the Lord. When the last scene of my life flashed before us, I looked back at the footprints in the sand. I noticed that many times along the path of my life, there was only one set of footprints.

I also noticed that it happened at the very lowest and saddest times in my life this really bothered me, and I questioned the Lord about it. "Lord, you said that once I decided to follow you, you would walk with me all the way; but I have noticed that during the most troublesome times in my life, there is only one set of footprints. I don't understand why in times when I needed you the most, you should leave me.

The Lord replied, "My precious, precious child. I love you, and I would never, never leave you during your times of trial and suffering. When you saw only one set of footprints, it was then that I carried you.

Globe Trotting
I try – Macy Gray
ⓓ

At 20, I took a flight to Thailand with my friends, my Mum and Stepdad Derrick; to visit Mum's friend. She was working in Thailand and we took the opportunity to see her, catch up and explore the beautiful country.

We were introduced to some of her Thai friends. This was the best thing ever as we got to see the *real* Thailand. We stayed in a place called Hua Hin. It is a coastal town and I had the most amazing experience.

I became close to a Thai boy called Ooui. He was very sweet, and I rode around Hua Hin on the back of his Moped, side-saddle, like a true native. We would all go to the Mountains to drink Sangsom Thai Whiskey, play the guitar and watch the sunrise.

One morning Ooui took me to the beach to see and experience a breath-taking sunrise. At this time, we would also see the Buddhist monks that walked along the beach as they received their offerings from the locals, we also collected food and presented it to them. It was such a humbling moment and the monks gave us a blessing in return.

I believe this holiday started something for all of us; It took me a little longer to get the travel bug, but a stale relationship gave me the motivation I needed.

At this stage in my life I worked for British Airways in a very exciting role at Heathrow Airport in terminal 1, 2 and 4. I looked after the queries from the VIPs in the Concorde and First Lounges. I remember making one very excited call to my Mum telling her that Richard Gere had just held the door open for me!

On another morning I had a chat with Bob Holness of *BlockBusters Fame*. It took all my willpower not to say, "Can I have a P please Bob?!"

At this time, I was living with a boyfriend who whilst I was working hard, he was sleeping hard. I'm not sure if it was the job that got to me in the end, or the boyfriend, or maybe it was because I had gotten bored? But I was ready for my next challenge....

This boyfriend was my first serious relationship. As I think back, I'm not entirely sure how I feel about it or whether my memories are fond ones. I definitely feel as though he clipped my wings. I had dreams and visions of a life that would inspire me and allow me to be free with my creative thoughts and thinking.

I have always struggled to fit neatly into the box of another person's ideas. I am not one to conform; not knowingly or intentionally rebelling nor creating waves, just quietly deferring from the path and walking my own route.

I am not happy when I feel that I am unable to walk the path that is secretly guiding me and pulling me.

So, encouraged by my Mum, I saved hard and worked three jobs. I now had my fulltime job at Whitbread, an evening job at a Pub and a Saturday job in a men's clothes shop.

I left the controlling lacklustre relationship, the boyfriend and grabbed my rucksack and took a flight to Australia, to meet up with my friend. My adventure began, I was off.

I was free!

I waved goodbye to my Dad at Gatwick airport and ventured through to the departure lounge; feeling footloose and fancy free, I was ready for new experiences. After a very long flight, many transfers and delays. I landed at Sydney airport in November 1999; tired and super jet lagged.

My friend met me and took me back to our pad; a rented house in Bondi. *Wow!*

Bondi Beach. I remember the weather being crazy. Before I had arrived, they'd had a crazy hailstone storm and some of the cars and houses were still showing signs of damage. It was bloody cold and not what I had expected at all.

Going Solo
Deep Forest – Deep Forest
(▷)

I spent some time in Sydney. I celebrated my birthday with a Lebanese Meal and tickets to the Ballet at the Sydney Opera House. Thank you to my friend for that beautiful birthday experience which will be forever etched in my memory. My family back home sent over cards, gifts and money and I was really grateful for all the effort they had made.

After a short while in the house I started to feel bored. Unfortunately (or fortunately) I didn't really get on with the housemates we were living with. It was not that we didn't get on; I guess we just had different agendas. They were all working in the CBD (Central Business District) and looking to settle for a long time and maybe gain sponsorship. I, on the other hand, was there for a good time on a tourist visa. And so, after a trip to the Blue Mountains and some very drunken nights, I decided it was best for me to go off on my merry way.

I bought myself a ticket for the Greyhound Buses and went solo to a place called Fraser Island. This coach journey lasted *forever*. Finally, I arrived at a Hostel where I would rest for a couple of days, before I went on to Fraser Island.

Hostel Life was a very strange concept to get used to. I arrived in the dark to a room full of sleeping bodies and rucksacks. I think I bonded well with my roomies (not!). They instantly took a dislike to me when I faffed about with my stuff; rustling carrier bags and what not, while they were trying to sleep. I opted for no eye contact the next morning!

Fraser Island was simply amazing. I met a great group of people and we travelled well together. I loved the feeling of survival and seeing snakes for the first time was a reminder that I was very far from England. I swam in crystal-clear creeks and walked along white sandy beaches. I remember a moment when time stood still; I sat alone by Lake Wobby and cleansed my soul. It was a very Spiritual moment. I literally felt any negative energy that had been stored within me and all those feelings of sadness from my relationship and all those feelings of frustration and repression just melt away. Lake Wobby cleansed my entire being.

I took my turn in driving the big 4x4, dodging snakes and rocks scattered along the beaches. We used our Eski (cooler box) lids to propel ourselves at speed down the sand dunes. As we set up camp before dark and settled in for the night, with a nice 'warm' glass of wine in my hand and some snags on the *barbie*, we listened to the dingoes calling each other and howling like wolves.

This trip was medicine for my soul. I cleansed my Spirit and rejuvenated myself. I could not have felt any more liberated. I'm pretty sure I could get used to life on a Desert Island. Although these days, I would definitely need a few more home comforts; a soft mattress, proper toilets and a shower. Oh… and a COLD glass of wine!

Next stop was Byron Bay. This was where I spent most of my Australian adventure. I stayed in the dorms at first and then camped once my friend arrived. The hostel was called The Arts

Factory. It was a hippy heaven and I felt very content; plenty of didgeridoos, barefooting and dreadlocks.

We pitched up a tent and we called that 'Home' for the next six weeks. Amazingly, that little tent sheltered us from some crazy rainforest storms, despite it being a bit wonky. The toilets in the camping area were very rustic. So rustic in fact, there was a huge snake! It was a carpet python and harmless. It had taken up residency and made itself quite comfortable coiled up in the rafters. Every time I had a pee, the snake was only a metre or so from my eye line. Oddly, I found I was cool with that; I think Fraser Island had prepared me for this and I had become accustomed to the wilderness and wild things.

Christmas time in Australia was strange for me, I felt really miserable. Christmas time should be *cold*. I don't want hot sunshine on Christmas Day. I need grey, rainy, cold or even at a push snowy weather. What I had was a scorching, hot day on the beach. Not a turkey in sight for dinner just backpacker, vegetarian delights. And to top it all, I didn't have anywhere to hang my lovely cards and gifts I had received from home. I don't think the stonking bender I went on that Christmas Eve helped either. No amount of Bourbon could help me through and rescue my sombre mood... But by Boxing Day, I was over my misery and back to the happy highs of backpacker life.

I met an Ozzie whilst I was in Byron Bay. He was gorgeous. Tall, slim and toned with long blond wavy hair. He was a proper surfer dude. As soon as we met, we just clicked. We met in the launderette and started chatting. For some reason I was instantly at ease with him; he laughed at my jokes, there was definitely some chemistry sparking between us. We ended up hanging out quite a bit and would stroll into town together.

One night, we had been out drinking with a group of people and the good times continued back at the hostel and well into the night. People gradually disappeared, and it was just the two of us. We talked about everything and anything; just deep meaningful conversation. We chatted and hugged until the sun rose.

Although nothing happened, I was so freaked out by how close I felt to him, I hid from him the next day!

Knowing I had a toxic relationship back home, it felt worse because we had connected on a deeper level, I felt as though I had cheated, but I hadn't. I stayed in my dorm all the next day and read. What a wally!

It's amazing how close you can feel to another person just by talking, really talking properly. That's what I need in my life and have always needed; conversations with substance. Nothing gets me more, than chewing over the world with someone.

New Year's Eve 1999

1999 – Prince

According to the media this was to be one of the most significant events of our century. People feared that once the clock struck midnight, all the computers would malfunction, all modern-day luxuries would be destroyed, and we'd be forced to live in the dark ages. But the 'Y2K Disaster' never materialised.

On New Year's Eve 1999, there was the most dramatic thunderstorm in Byron Bay. This only contributed to the fear that the world was about to end! So, in true backpacker style we drank and smoked our way through this uncertainty. There was a group of us who had bonded together; we were all lone travellers and we just clicked. I remember one girl from London (who was older and also escaping a dead-end relationship), another girl from Massachusetts and two other girls from Liverpool. There were others, but these were the main group I'd been hanging out with.

Finally, the storm settled and we ventured into the town and partied like it was 1999! It was a long night; the hangovers were hellish, but that aside we did witness the first sunrise of the new Millennium. I will never forget that very first sunrise in the year 2000. It gave me hope and dreams of a future so alive with opportunities. The world was my oyster.

I started the New Year cleansing my soul from the hard partying of New Year's Eve. We visited Minion Falls, a beautiful waterfall. It was all very lovely and refreshing, apart for the leeches that took a shine to me!

I had leeches attached to my legs, feet and ankles. I don't know how, but I was very calm about it and just flicked the little blighters off me. Bear Grylls would have been proud, I'm sure. The amount of blood that followed however was not pretty.

Red Mountain; It's a New Year, a New Day and a New Dawn.

"Feel the blossom around you, as your words take flight. No one is mightier than the Spirit that lives within you. Everyone is searching for that special way of existing, of living and of being. Yet is there anything more spectacular than that of "just being you?

There are too many external influences in your world, that alter the state of mind and the state of being. That so seldom is man truly, his authentic identity.

He can take on so many characteristics and be so many people to many different friends - that no one truly knows who this man is, not even himself.

It is only when you commit to living by the rules of the earth and commit to a life of guidance from your own inner voice, that you will find that peace to be who you are "meant" to be.

Unlike the many others, when you walk your own path, to your own beat, unaffected by the vibrations of the characters that surround you - you will find your true peace.

It is not for you to judge those that have not found their peace, for this is their own journey. Nor must you mock if you see flaws in their story. Accept with blessings - until such time that your path should meet again.

EXPLORATION

Those that mock your journey may do so, as a consequence of naivety. Allow them their voice and smile with peace in your heart. You have nothing to prove, content with wisdom in your soul. Life is an adventure across many lifetimes. Cherish your inner wisdom, for not all are blessed with this knowledge this time around."

Thailand & Vietnam
Natural Blues - Moby

I spent a few more days into the New Year in Oz, then moved on to South East Asia; stopping for a short while in Bangkok and then flying to Vietnam.

Our hostel in Bangkok was dark and dingy. If you have ever seen the film *Bangkok Hilton*, it felt a little like this. It was very basic with bare wires exposed and a mattress on the floor. There was a lot of hustle and bustle where we were staying just off the Khaosan Road in Bangkok. When I arrived, I bumped into an old school friend and spent a few days with him, what a small world!

We stayed long enough to visit Wat Pho, 'The Temple of the Reclining Buddha'. It's absolutely amazing; a giant reclining Buddha that measures 46 metres long and is covered in gold leaf.

We also arranged our visas for Laos, then took a flight out of Bangkok to Vietnam.

The flight to Vietnam was memorable as we boarded this tiny plane full of Vietnamese people. A lot of the other passengers stared at us! They all had little pots of noodles and sat and munched their way through the short flight.

Arriving in Ho Chi Minh City, we changed our money and in return were handed a stack of notes that was about 30cm high. We jumped in a taxi and drove to our Guesthouse, Miss Loi's. On the way, we were literally swarmed by Vietnamese people, looking through the windows, pointing at us, touching the glass. This was quite an experience. Miss Loi soon calmed things down by welcoming us. Miss Loi and several of her 'girls' as she referred to them were all dressed in silk nightwear.

Where were we? What sort of place was this?

Any doubts or fears were soon alleviated when we were offered coffees and bananas; coffee brought to us in beautiful glasses, sweet and milky.

When we prepared to venture out for the night, we were warned not to have our bags on show, as these would be cut off by a passing moped. It was difficult to stomach seeing all the dogs in cages along the sides of the street; snakes, dogs and god knows what else were on the menu. I remained a committed vegetarian during my stay in Vietnam.

Whilst we were there, we visited the War Remnants Museum in Ho Chi Minh City. This was a very sad place to visit. We learned exactly what the Vietnamese had experienced during the war. We left feeling very sombre.

Away from the harshness of the city, we booked a boat trip to cruise along the Mekong Delta. Sailing down the river in a longboat, 'Go' by Moby was the soundtrack for this journey. Listening to that Album takes me back to the beauty of the sunset and the orange sky. My emotions at that time were of pure amazement at the beauty which surrounded me. I was tearful and had feelings of enlightenment and was at total peace.

My thoughts went back to the Vietnam War as I also imagined the red sky being filled with helicopters. I felt as though I was connecting to the many memories and emotions of lost souls that had ended their journeys in this region. There was a stillness in the air and a warmth that carried sadness.

This calmness in my trip was suddenly interrupted and in true reflection, a perfect example of my lack of attention to detail on the big things in life...

I ran out of money and was forced to cut my trip short! No trip to Laos for me. What came next was a whole heap of worry as I had to spend the next 48 hours in Bangkok Airport, trying desperately to arrange a flight home.

The reversed charges phone call to my Mum went something like this...

"Mum, I'm not in any trouble, *but* I've run out of money and can't get a flight home!"

I survived on a Baguette and *Dairylea* triangle for the next 48 hours in Bangkok airport. I made friends with another backpacker and felt so guilty leaving her when my flight was eventually sorted.

I boarded that Thai Airways flight back to Heathrow, ordered a large Whiskey, then fell asleep for the rest of the journey, with my head on the tray table.

It was a shock to the system, arriving home to the English Winter in flip-flops and a summer skirt. My Mum collected me from the Airport and it felt so good to finally be home.

BELONGING

We look to try and find the place where we belong.

Mr. Rich
Hallelujah – Jeff Buckley

I returned home and began living with Mum and Derrick again.

Whilst I was away, my mind was clear, and I knew what I had to do about my unhealthy relationship. But it was too easy to sink back into the familiarity of a relationship with my boyfriend. Thankfully, it didn't last much longer, and we called it a day.

I soon moved out of my Mum's and began house-sharing with a friend.

I worked at *Whitbread's* as a temp after leaving BA, staying for the next six years. The only reason I lasted that long was because I left twice; once to go travelling and they took me back and once to go to the glistening bright lights of an exciting new role which I hated and abruptly did a U-turn and went back. Thankfully, my lovely Manager, sympathised with my flighty character and accepted me back.

My last stint was in Marketing. It was an exciting role and I enjoyed the job. I was working as a Packaging and Design Executive, so it fulfilled my creative side... But unfortunately, it would never have worked out as I just didn't fit it.

It was obvious what I had to do; I handed in my notice – with no job lined up.

One good thing to come out of my time at Whitbread's, was my friendship with Nic. We would have fag breaks together and chat about anything and everything. I think we actually started on the same day. I am still good friends with Nic now. I asked her about her thoughts on my connection to Spirit, and this is what she had to say...

"My lovely friend Nic... We have a friendship that I treasure. We've known each other for about 20 years. Wow! Watched each other grow into adults and mothers. Early on in our friendship we often moaned and discussed our young love woes. But as we got older our chats moved to marriage and family.

We used to speak a lot of the Spirit world, and visited a lovely German medium, we were so excited after it and talked a lot about the other side. As the years went on; jobs changed; life took us in different directions, we lost touch at times but always found each other. When I knew you'd taken your Spirituality to a different level I was very proud and in awe. I never had the courage to do it... And now you're writing, doing something you love!

You've grown into a remarkable person; powerful, sensitive, strong and a very good friend. I think it will be a bright and sparkling future."

-

I spent the next few years partying and going to festivals; *Glastonbury, V Festival* & *Reading, Knebworth* and the *Oasis* concert. The concert of all concerts! My goodness that was proper Rock and Roll. We partied hard! Liam and Noel would have been proud, I'm sure. Only we partied a bit *too* hard.   Me and my friend lost everyone and had to call my Dad at about 3am to come and take us home! Thanks Dad.

Seeing live bands was my main hobby. I saw *The Who, The Rolling Stones, Pink Floyd, James Brown, UB40* and many more.

Looking for some calm, I took a trip to Switzerland with Mum and Derrick to visit Derrick's brother. It was such a cleansing trip. The place is so crisp and clean. I remember a boat trip across Lake Lucerne and the time we spent at the top of the Mountains, feeding the huge blackbirds from my hands. It was certainly good for my soul. When I returned, as much as I had enjoyed the crazy times and the parties, I was so ready to meet my Rob in 2002.

I was out with Emma J and we were celebrating her birthday, so it was 15th June 2002. Emma and I were in a pub chatting when I noticed Rob walk in with his friends. We locked eyes immediately and I felt an instant knowing. We didn't speak but I think I waved to his friends, as I knew some of them. It was the time of the World Cup and spirits were high; I think England had been playing that day.

Emma and I finished our drinks and went our separate ways. I started to walk home but decided to take a detour and went into another pub on the way. Well thank God I did, as Rob was in there, we started chatting and it was easy right from the start. Day became night and we stayed together as his friends left, going on to a club.

There was nothing complicated about Rob, what you see is what you get. We clicked straightaway and from that moment I knew we would marry (although I obviously didn't tell him this or he would've run a mile!)

Rob was, and still is, the one for me. After all the 'relationships' I'd had in the past, none had ever been quite like this. He was kind and a gentleman; he took care of me unlike anyone before. It was the little things that really made a difference. I would come home after work and find that he had washed up for me and turned on the heating and lights. Making things cosy for me and that's exactly what I needed in my life!

When Rob came along with his homely, cosy, comforting ways, and started to take care of me, I fell head over heels in love with him. I settled into my life with him with gratitude. I was ready for some calm.

When we first met, Rob said that he was drawn to my free spirit and independence. He said that he knew instantly that I wasn't just an average girl, he knew that I had a massive heart and was very special.

Initially, I think he found it all a bit intimidating. He would come to my house which would be candlelit. Me and my housemate and friends would drink gallons of wine and he'd be immersed in the girls' night in. I think he could handle it to a point but when we moved the coffee table to dance or laid on the floor like starfish and listened to Jeff Buckley's *Hallelujah* a lot; that took a lot of getting used to. Even now with my friends, Tony and Vic, it will get to a certain point in the evening and the coffee table will get moved to allow for some drunken dancing.

Rob believes that having my Guides in my life has helped me become an even better person. He has said that he can see how they have guided me and given me direction.

Rob is pretty openminded, but it has been a bit of a struggle for him to see me flit about from one job to another. He knows that it has been hard for me, but I don't think he has really understood the burning desire I have had; the need to look for something more and knowing that there is more to life, my way of thinking is often too big for him. For him, he wanted to go to work, do his job, then come home and relax.

Therefore, I have been a big source of frustration for him sometimes and turned his little world upside down and on its head... As I have always said to him, "Put your sneakers on, we're going on an adventure!"

Many times, he has been happy to put his sneakers on. I believe he trusts me, but not only me, now he trusts Spirit. He trusts my Guide, Red Mountain, who has been by my side for many years now. But more importantly we share the same philosophy in that if something isn't right, we go ahead and change it; including the big things, like jobs and houses.

He doesn't pass judgement and has never given any thoughts or opinions on my development, but he has shared my excitement when something very breath-taking has happened.

In particular, I have given Rob messages from his Dad, who I never met. By me explaining his Dad's character in the message, and highlighting how he stood back, and his mannerisms, this was all the convincing Rob needed. Along with also giving Rob a message from a close friend that he lost in his teenage years. This has changed Rob's opinions and views enormously. This made him a Believer.

Rob and I have always shared a love of music and he continues to make me laugh as much as he ever did. This sense of humour has carried us through some very shitty, testing times.

Red Mountain has said...

"You work well together, you have struggled, and it has been hard. Harder than you realise, you have been tested, but your love is strong. Be kind to one another, he is your soul mate. Your differences complement each other, you may find he is a little un- motivated at times, but he keeps you grounded. He is real and genuine, an old soul, and he loves you."

Journey of Development

Very Superstitious – Stevie Wonder

ⓘ

After a little time, Rob and I were forced to move in together, due to a nightmarish house-share situation.

We moved to Flitwick and rented a cute little house. From there we bought our first house in Houghton Regis; a two-bed terrace and along came Ginger George and Cleo, our cats.

At this time, I was working in Recruitment. Apart from being bored with the role, I was also frustrated with the 'corporate' way of life.

This was when I began to put more emphasis on my development as I saw it as a way to escape the boredom and monotony. My only respite from the corporate *blah-blah*, were my work friends Webbo and Jammin. The laughs that we had seemed to make it all so much more bearable.

Initially I was bought a pack of Angel Cards and I began to use them regularly; really connecting with the cards and loving their energy. The energy of these cards was light and encouraging. I had wanted to stay away from Tarot Cards at that stage as I felt they were darker and heavier.

These cards guided me, and I took notice of the messages I was receiving. They guided me onto further study and I took an Open University course called 'Open to Change'.

This course helped me a lot, as it made me realise that my tendency to change my mind and alter my direction was not necessarily such a negative thing, as I had always been told by family. What I began to realise was that it was actually positive. This changed my viewpoint and I began to believe that anything was possible, and change can bring many opportunities.

I have always connected really well with my Cards. This set was actually bought for me by my Mum's Mother. She was always that way inclined, particularly with Angels or so she had me believe. We always treated her as though she was special. This would go on to change as I learnt more about the torment within the family. I am a little unsure about what was true back then and what wasn't. My history and memories are now extremely fragmented.

Anyway, I digress, back to the Angel Cards... They are a light, gentle tool to help me interpret messages from my Guides, Spirit helpers and Angels. By using a deck of cards, I can ask questions and receive answers, laying them out in different positions and reading the messages.

Once I started using these cards, I didn't look back. They became a stable part of my life, and I followed the guidance I was receiving with trust. I believe it is often the case; Angel Cards are given to you and end up finding their way to you, rather than you actively seeking them out.

In the beginning I was quite slow in reading the cards, but they came with a little booklet which helped me to translate the cards and their meanings. So, I would shuffle the cards and ask the deck my question in my head or out loud, it didn't really matter, and I would pick out the cards I was drawn to. Picking with the non-dominant hand is often a good technique as it is more driven by your subconscious.

Three cards give a really quick overview of the past, present and future. At this stage in my life the readings that came through often directed me to more learning and more meditation. Therefore, that is exactly what I did...

As I became more confident with the cards, I naturally started to understand the messages and intuition would give me more than what was written in the book. I would end up hearing words popping into my head and felt a very good connection with these cards. I still use them now. They are a little frayed around the edges; well used.

These are the same cards that I started to give readings with, initially to family, then friends and then at Psychic Fairs. These cards are very positive and encouraging; never negative. They give comfort and quite often encourage tears. I always used to find, that the tears allowed the person receiving the reading to move on.

I'd find that many people were stuck in their emotions and I was helping them to release their inner blockages. It allowed people to really free themselves from feelings that were making them feel sad or trapped. I always had a box of tissues on my table when working, because people would release their tears with me and leave feeling lighter.

I had a friend that I worked with at *Whitbread*, Davinia. She and I got on so well. At work, we chatted absolute rubbish to get us through a day of Data Entry. We would also get together often to give each other a reading. She would use her Fairy Cards and I would use my Angel Cards; we'd merge our cards together and get some fantastic in-depth readings. Davinia and I had a great friendship on a 'soul level'. She was just like Phoebe from *Friends* and I loved the way she lives her life. I was a bridesmaid at her wedding but then we lost contact for many years but thankfully, we have reconnected recently.

-

To receive my daily message, I would draw a card. If I was unsure about anything and needed direction, happy or sad, I would use the cards. They gave me so much and spring- boarded me into developing further.

After a while I began to use another set; this time it was a dowsing set using cards, pendulum and meditations. This set took my development to another level as it was working more with the Archangels. I had some very mind-blowing meditations with the Archangels and colour during this stage, and I was in a place of amazement. I could feel that things were changing enormously. My world was changing, and my mind was opening. I would feel the wings of the Archangels embracing me with warmth and security which at times would feel overwhelming; full of emotion, tears would fall down my cheeks during meditation.

Michael is the Archangel that gives protection; during this period I was working for a Housing Authority and I would ask for the Archangels for protection every morning before going into the office. I would visualise Michael's heavy dark blue cloak being wrapped around my shoulders and wrapping me from head to toe. I would ask that he protected me from any negativity. Once I had completed this ritual, I would feel ready to face the office and the negativity that was waiting for me.

The Archangels are always there, ready to help but they will not interfere; it is essential that you ask them to help you. Once you have instructed them to work with you, they will be right by your side.

Archangel Raphael is the Angel of Healing. I would call on him and ask for help when I needed extra healing or healing for my friends and family. I would ask him to draw close and surround me in his green healing light.

I would share these experiences with Rob and during his time of being made redundant, we both focussed intently on positivity and put our faith in the Angels. Rob in particular, would reach out to Archangel Ithuriel and Zadkiel. Rob ended up with a better job at a very good company which gave him the opportunity to learn a good trade. Our faith didn't falter during this time of uncertainty, it was as though it was all in hand. I believe he still turns to them, to this day, when he needs some extra support; he will put his thoughts out to them and ask for their help.

Counselling

Something Inside So Strong – Labbi Siffre
(▷)

Looking back on my childhood, I had always been a good listener. I had to absorb and soak up the world around me. So, an interest in counselling was pretty obvious. I guess this was the start of my career, as it is today.

I went to college to learn how to listen to people properly. This is an actual art. There are so many people that listen but do not hear. Listening is about hearing the spoken word but also hearing what is *unspoken*.

There is so much to be said in the way someone uses their tone of voice. How do they pitch those words; are they quiet, calm, loud or agitated? How does the person sit or stand as they explain their story? What does their body language and gestures say? The expressions on a person's face and how they look are vital. Do they give eye contact or look into the distance? Does a person talk with their hands?

Once you stop talking and allow someone the space to talk, amazing things happen. Quite often people do not get the chance to talk uninterrupted and be allowed the space and time to reveal more about themselves and their story.

As a sensitive person, I'm aware I have great empathy and I am able to put myself in someone else's position. I may even have had a similar experience that I can draw on that will help me to absorb myself in the details that are being shared. As a sensitive, quite often I feel too much and can absorb some of the emotions felt by other people. This can leave me feeling quite tired and drained at times. Often feeling as though I may need to retreat for a while to rebuild my energies.

Having empathy for other people is a skill I know I can rely on. Empathy allows me to really connect to a person on a 'soul level', whilst they tell their story.

As a counsellor it is essential that I am naturally accepting of other people and their journeys. I must be able to listen without judgement. I will not always agree with everyone or with what they are saying. However, to have the art of listening without judgment, is something quite special. It also saves me the feeling of needing or wanting to change other people, and just allow them to walk their own path; that was intended for them.

Part of the satisfaction of working with people, is being able to use my communication skills and really choose my words carefully, use words that really matter to me. How I say things and the tone that I use, is incredibly important, even the written word. In this day and age, when we use messaging, tweets and Facebook so readily, it's really important to use the right words. In counselling even more so, as it's about building a relationship of trust and openness and it's essential to break down any barriers to enable my clients to feel at ease.

Knowing that life transforms and that people can change has helped me to counsel others. Quite often a client will have a fixed viewpoint, only to change this way of thinking in the next breath. It is imperative that I move with the ebb and flow of life and encourage my clients to do the same. If everything were so rigid, it would just snap with the next gust of wind.

Meditation

Tibetan Meditation Music Nawang Khechog
(▷)

During this time, I began to meditate every day. Each evening I would connect with the Archangels and they would envelop me in their wings as I sat, meditating.

Initially I would follow a guided meditation. Using my Dowsing Angel Meditation pack and the cards that prompted me through meditation with the Angels. I would sit in my quiet room with candles and incense; setting the scene for meditation is imperative. To try and create calm when you are surrounded by chaos is never gonna happen!

If you are not blessed to have a room for Meditation, you can dedicate a corner of your room, or a shelf, to your sacred meditation space. What is important to you? For me it was, and still is, a candle and some nature, a plant or flowers and a Buddha for inspiration and always some scent. Scent is very important for me as it will take me to a faraway place, whether it be incense sticks or a room spray, it doesn't matter but I think it helps enormously. Sometimes I use music, but mostly I sit in silence. I find that music can be a distraction.

I would sit in a chair or on the floor with cushions and I would tell Rob not to disturb me.

To begin I would close my eyes concentrate on just my breathing for a while, then I would begin to follow the guidance of the Angel Card Meditations. They would take me off to a beautiful place to meet with the Angels and Archangels and that is where I would stay maybe for an hour or so. My breathing would slow down, and I would enter a state of just *being*.

When I began to teach Meditation, people would often say to me; "I can't Meditate because I can't stop my thoughts."

This is the first barrier, and this stops so many people from trying to Meditate. Please understand we are never trying to *stop* these endless thoughts. We are merely trying to create a bigger gap between each thought. As soon as people realise that this is not the objective, they calm down, sit back and begin to enjoy the ride. The more you meditate the easier it becomes, and the brain begins to learn the new way of being, and new patterns are created.

By week 8, (there is scientific evidence to prove this) there will be changes within your brain and the benefits will be life changing. Yes, *seriously*; it is that amazing! I've seen it happen time and time again. But like anything worthwhile, it takes time and dedication.

During my Meditation in this stage in my life, I would visualize colours so beautiful; purples, reds, greens and blues. I can never begin to explain in enough detail just how beautiful these colours would appear. The colours were so intense. They'd give me healing and add multiple layers of depth to my meditation. It was an experience that can only be felt, not explained.

I would see a psychedelic mix of moving colour. For my development and confirmation of connection I would see a purple that had life to it. If you have ever tried Acid, I think this is the closest way to explain these images of colour. Truly beautiful and breath-taking.

I would see green for healing. A green that felt so alive, the greenest of plants, as though I could almost smell the scent of cut grass.

Yellow, as bright as the sunshine; almost golden and blinding with light.

From seeing colour, I moved on to seeing symbols. The first images I saw would be eagles and anchors.

-

Eagle Symbolism:

As a power animal, the Eagle is most frequently associated with wisdom and freedom. Here are additional symbolic meanings for the Eagle totem: Intuition, Creativity, Strength, Courage, Hope, Resilience, Healing, Vision and Healing.

(source: http://www.Spiritanimal.info/eagle-Spirit-animal/)

The Anchor symbolises:

An anchor is a heavy weight that holds a ship in place. Remaining firm and steadfast amid the uncertainty of storms and the elements, an anchor symbolizes such concepts as firmness, tranquillity and hope.

(source: http://www.religionfacts.com/anchor)

Colour Therapy & Chakras

Misty Blue – Dorothy Moore

ⓘ

The next obvious choice for me, after seeing the colours during my Meditation, was a Diploma in Colour Therapy. My dream was to make a career for myself, in which I had the freedom to work around having children.

I'd be self-employed. I had always hoped that I'd be able to build a business with the notion that I could abandon the Monday to Friday, 9 to 5 life. I had wanted to be there for my child and I really did not want him to ever have to let himself in from school.

What is Colour Therapy?

Colour Therapy is a complementary therapy for which there is evidence backing up its healing properties, dating back thousands of years to the ancient cultures of Egypt, China and India.

Colour Therapy and its theories are based on the Principles of the Chakra system. Seven spectrums of colour, consisting of red, orange, yellow, green, blue, indigo and violet, each colour resonating with the energy of each of the chakras/energy centres of the body. Try to imagine the chakras as a set of wheels, each wheel needs to spin smoothly for the body to work effectively. Optimum health and wellbeing are achieved by balancing all of these energies. Colour Therapy can help to re-balance and restore these energy centres by applying the appropriate colour to the body and therefore re-balancing the chakras.

Colour is absorbed in many ways - by the eyes, the skin, and our 'magnetic energy field' or aura and the energy of colour affects us on many levels, emotionally, physically, mentally, and holistically. There are many different techniques for giving a colour treatment. These can include: a treatment using solarised water, or using light boxes/lamps with colour filters, coloured silks and hands on healing using a treatment of colour visualisation.

-

The way that I used colour initially was with my Reiki treatments I would visualise the colour of each chakra as I worked on that energy centre during the Reiki treatment. Then, I began to understand the meaning of wearing certain colours and how it affects moods and emotions.

I went on to use colour when I was teaching Meditation. I always found it to be particularly powerful and people responded well to the Colour Meditations.

Reiki

Hey There, Delilah – Plain White T's

ⓘ

The next stage for me was Reiki. I signed up for my *Reiki 1 Attunement*. I was still following guidance and attending a Spiritual centre in Dunstable, I was being led to this next level of development.

What is The Attunement?

Reiki is not taught in the way other healing techniques are taught. It is transferred to the student from the Reiki Master during an Attunement process. This process opens the crown, heart, and palm chakras and creates a special link between the student and the Reiki (Energy) source.

The Reiki Attunement is a very powerful spiritual experience. The process is guided from Reiki Masters who have lived long beforehand and they will make adjustments in the Attunement, depending on the needs of each individual student. The Attunement, is attended by Reiki guides and other Spiritual beings who help implement the process. Many students will report having mystical experiences involving personal messages, healings, visions, and past life experiences. The Attunement will increase psychic ability and openness to Spirit.

Once you have received a Reiki Attunement, you will have Reiki forever. It does not wear off and you will never lose it.

The Reiki Attunement can begin a cleansing process that affects the physical body as well as the mind and emotions. Toxins that have been stored in the body may be released along with feelings and thought patterns that are no longer useful. Therefore, it is highly recommended that a process of purification prior to the Attunement is applied, to gently prepare you for this Attunement.

Unfortunately, I was not given this advice beforehand and I certainly wish I had of been. After my Reiki 1 I was ok. But I had a very strange experience after Level 2 and Master Level; I was not in a good place, it took me a very long time to get back on track.

Recently I was asked if I teach Reiki or if I could recommend a teacher. This is not something I feel comfortable in recommending. Because my experience was so intense, I would always hesitate to suggest any guidance on a person's Reiki path. I feel it is very individualised and dependent on so many aspects. If it is right for you, you will find the right teacher.

I describe my Attunement as, *'intense'*. The Reiki Master worked behind me, with me in Meditation; she took me to a level I had not experienced before.

I went to a place that was certainly in another realm, another atmosphere; I guess it could also be described as an out of body experience. Then I was brought back and sent on my merry way; into the big world, into town to get some lunch. I felt like only half of me was present and that I had left the other half of me in the outer realms.

I would urge you to choose your Reiki Teacher carefully and ensure that it is the right time in your life to go on this journey.

Please read up on all the information available and plan a "quiet" period for at least two days afterwards. I went so high, I was giddy and anxious. I confess it did get a little scary and it's clear that I really do have strong opinions on Reiki Attunements and how they are conducted.

We went back after lunch and practiced giving Reiki to each other. Things settled as the afternoon went on, but I was certainly not the same person as I was before, or ever again!

During this Reiki Attunement I had been inducted into the world of Reiki Symbols and healing. I was taught how to heal myself with the symbols, hand sequences and positions.

This heightened my sense of Spirituality, deepened my connection to my own journey, and undoubtedly helped in the next stage of my life. I began to offer Reiki to family and friends and my Meditation Room became my Treatment Room.

I would prepare the room in the same way I would for Meditation. I would ask for my Guides and helpers to step forward. I would ask for Reiki Masters past and present to join in the session, protecting me and my client and working only in the highest of good at all times.

Each treatment would vary. Clients could leave with a pillow face... You know, that face when you have just woken up from the deepest of sleeps; when you cannot care less about your expression and you may have awesome bed hair. This happens when the client has allowed themselves to relax to a level that has taken them so deep, it felt like they had slept for weeks.

As I have knowledge of the Chakras and the imbalances within the chakras and what the meanings are, I'd be able to tap into the subconscious of my client and work on their emotional wellbeing, as well as the physical.

As with all of the work that I do, the Holistic ethos runs deep, and I have always believed that thoughts and emotions can have a huge impact on physical wellbeing. This is the thinking behind the philosophies and teachings of the Chakra System.

I had one client come to me for some Reiki; she was actually an old school friend and I had not seen her since I was about 13. She had recently lost her Dad and she needed some help working through her grief.

We did a course of treatment that helped her to process her emotions. I believe I really did help her. I also believe the reason she came to me was because her Dad had wanted to send her a message.

-

At this time, I was also attending workshops for developing my mediumship. During one workshop, I received a message from one of the other learners, telling me that she had a father with her and he had two daughters. She went on to give me a message for my client. It was a short message of comfort, to let his daughter know that he was ok and had passed over peacefully. I delivered the message and his hopes were fulfilled. Spirit have a way of getting their messages through in any way they can.

Another client found the experience very unusual. He had many aches and pains and was willing to try something different. He went away feeling rejuvenated and has continued to rave about the effects he felt. He said it felt as though my hands were on fire, they were so hot with the healing energy pumping through them. His other comment was that it felt as though another pair of hands was working with me, as when I was working on his knees he felt a pair of hands on his feet.

This is often the case with healing. These are the hands of Spirit healers.

I had another lady that came to me for a course of treatment; each week she snored her head off. I'm used to people falling asleep on me. I think she was unsure if it was working. But I know it was working, because if you are that relaxed to fall deeply asleep with a stranger, then you are receiving exactly what you need, and this lady undoubtedly needed to relax.

Reiki will always give you exactly what you need. You may feel as though you are needing healing on your shoulder, when in actual fact you are needing some deep relaxation to help ease the tension that you are storing in your shoulder.

BECOMING

We enter the real world of an adult life, led by the Heart and learn how to refine and effectively invest in our own emotions.

Marriage

Les Nuits – Nightmares on Wax
ⓘ

Rob and I married on 19th June 2006 in Cyprus. At this stage in my life, I was in a very good place with my spirituality. I knew in my heart what was meant to be.

I look back now and I'm glad that my Spirituality carried me through my wedding day. My Dad wasn't able to attend or give me away. So, my Mum took his place and walked me down the aisle to 'Les Nuits' by Nightmares on Wax.

A beautiful moment that I will always think back on with happiness; walking down the aisle with cream butterflies flying all around us.

—

Now here's a thing, at the time I believed that the sole reason my Dad was unable to give me away was because his back was bad. It was a fact that my Dad had always suffered with his back. Now that I am able to view things more holistically, I can certainly relate stress to his back problems.

What I hadn't realised was that the stress my Dad was under at that time, was monumental.

Asking the Impossible

Wish I Didn't Miss You – Angie Stone

▷

A few years ago, my Mum dropped the bombshell. My poor Mum exploded with the truth that she had been hiding for decades. At the time of my wedding this bombshell was still very much under wraps; the way her Father had preferred it to be.

Only Dad was very aware of what this bombshell was. So, asking him to come to my wedding and give me away, where he would have had to rub shoulders with my Mother's Father, seemed an impossible feat.

Okay here we go, this is not the easiest of things to divulge, so please bear with me… My Mum has been on a journey of courage and she finally found the strength from within to report her own Father for Sexual Abuse; abuse that continued from the age of 11 to 17. Her own Father robbed her of her innocence.

Not only do I hate my Mum's Father for what he has done to my Mum and the knock-on effect it has had on her & my life. I also hate this man for robbing me and my Dad, of one of the most treasured experiences in a girl's life. A Father giving his only daughter away at her wedding is a God-given right, and a special moment in a father-daughter relationship.

He stole that from me.

It has been a very difficult time for my Mother, myself, and my remaining family. This confession has divided the family and there have been some very difficult moments.

My Mum has been an inspiration and my estimations of her have grown enormously. I now also understand why she acted in ways which I just couldn't understand as a child. Everything became clearer when she spoke her truth.

Hopefully this will encourage others to enter their own journey of recovery.

999
Brown Eyed Girl – Van Morrison
ⓘ

In 2007 my Stepdad Derrick, had a stroke. I remember the phone call from my Mum as I was in the bath.

I rushed around to my Mum's to find the quick-response Ambulance already there. Derrick was sitting in the chair, he was unable to speak or move his arms. At this point we did not know what was wrong with him. What I did notice though, was the look of sheer panic and fear in Derrick's big brown Malteser-eyes.

We went to the Hospital and Derrick was assessed and given a bed. He'd had a stroke. I knew nothing about strokes and thought it was the same as a heart attack. As I know now it wasn't, a stroke is connected to the brain - not the heart.

Derrick stayed in hospital overnight and when we left him, he had that same look of deep routed fear in his eyes. He looked so vulnerable. We went to visit him the next morning and we realised the actual effects of this stroke…

Derrick was unable to talk, walk, eat, drink and take care of himself. We managed to get him in a wheelchair and took him to the canteen. As Derrick tried to talk, I remember the horror I felt, as he was unable to make any coherent sentences and ended up making a lot of mumbling sounds and noises. This really shocked me, but I tried to act calm about the situation, pretending that all was ok and not as frightening as it really was.

Derrick hadn't looked well to me for a while. I had noticed that he appeared to have a murky brown Aura around him. This had been troubling me and I had been asking Mum to make him go to the Doctor's. Unfortunately, he hadn't and we later realised that he'd had several mini strokes leading up to this big one.

Ten years later and after much Physiotherapy, he is able to walk again; although a bit wonky and with the use of a stick. His voice and speech are better but have never recovered fully, and when he gets really tired, it's very hard to understand him fully. But, on the flipside, Derrick and my Mum now have a much calmer lifestyle and they are closer than before. They are certainly enjoying their retirement years together.

Corby

I felt like there was NO music in my life at this time

ⓘ

I had always wanted and needed to distance myself from my Mum's side of the family, so when Rob's work offered relocation, we moved away.

We moved to Corby. I did the sensible thing and lined up a job in Northampton, as we prepared to move. What wasn't so sensible, was that I hadn't realised that Corby to Northampton was quite a drive for a low paid Admin role.

Derrick had experienced his stroke, I was already feeling the emotions of the trauma felt by him and my Mum, I had moved to a new home, new area, new job, decided to take my Reiki Master Level... I had a breakdown.

It didn't last long before I became ill, stressed and anxiety engulfed me, this was triggered by my Reiki Master Attunement. I ended up with severe anxiety and was unable to work, I felt alone and very unbalanced. I was an emotional wreck.

Years later, I looked back on this emotional upheaval and received a message from my Guide, Red Mountain...

Looking back at what happened to me...
"It was a breakdown my child, a shock to your system. You have limitations and you were pushing yourself too fast on your journey.

You did not allow your knowledge and heightened sense of worth to settle down. It was a way to make you stop and reassess things. The timing wasn't right for you to further your journey and you needed a break.

The experience has made you stronger and it has given you more knowledge and understanding of others.

You are a counsellor and you guide and help others; this experience has given you more credibility. Used as an example in your teaching. Your learners will have more of a connection with you and know that you are talking from experience. You will go from strength to strength. You will always guide and nurture but not always in the same way - I see you presenting to large audience's big workshops. You are gaining experience, you already have the coaching skills."

Following this, I seriously struggled to find any decent work.

Eventually I found a job in Recruitment and worked in the Avon factory, finding temporary workers. I didn't enjoy this, but one silver lining was that I did manage to study a Diploma in Life Coaching. I wasn't sure at the time how I was going to use it, but I completed it anyway and was awarded my diploma.

I was, however, still feeling lost and lonely, missing friends and family from Dunstable. We had a lovely house, but it was empty. There was no life in the house, no soul. If only we could have picked it up and transported it closer to Dunstable!

Anxiety & Panic Attacks
Wild World – Cat Stevens
ⓘ

Everyone experiences feelings of anxiety and panic at certain times. It's a natural response to stressful or dangerous situations. For me it had been a culmination of too many life changes all at once.

I was feeling so stressed and panic attacks were happening regularly and at any time, often for no apparent reason and without warning. I was afraid of everything.

Immediately after my Reiki Master Attunement, I felt disconnected. I went into town to meet friends and had to leave as I was unable to think straight.

That night I stayed at my Mum's house and it was a tough night. I felt like a sponge picking up on any tension and stress that surrounded me. I was like an exposed wire. My nerves were raw, and my eyes were wide; I was unable to switch off or unwind. I did not know what was happening to me.

The next morning after a night of no sleep, I went back to the Reiki Master for a treatment to try and ground me. This treatment did little to put me at ease. I was in an extremely vulnerable place. I needed to get back home to Corby and to Rob. Finally, I did arrive home, but I felt uneasy and worried constantly. I couldn't sleep or switch off. The next day I went to the Doctors and remember my feelings of being disconnected, even in the waiting room. I was not the same person.

I was afraid of feeling afraid. My fear would bring on panic attacks, and I was always worried, thus creating more panic attacks! I was in a vicious circle. I was even afraid of the medication I was prescribed so I didn't take it.

Panic attacks are horrible; your body experiences a rush of intense mental and physical stimulation. It can come on very quickly and for no reason. It's very frightening and scary.

For me I would experience a racing heartbeat, feel faint, inability to breathe properly, sometimes I would be so cold I'd be unable to warm up, dizziness and a feeling of dread as though I was about to die. My stomach would be in knots; feeling like my mind was not connected to my body.

I tried to calm this anxiety with Meditation and Reiki, as I preferred a natural route. I became a regular in Holland & Barrett; buying Valerian, a natural sleeping tablet, Lemon Balm for calming the heart and the body and Vitamin B12 for the nervous system. I had to work on my fear of Reiki, because I knew it was good for me. For a while, I doubted my Spiritual path. In reflection, it all calmed down once my life settled again, but it was always simmering just under the surface and that is one reason why I use meditation, to keep my anxiety at bay.

Even to this day, when things get hectic, I feel it rearing its head again; like a mean old friend. It's a sign that things need to calm down and I need to step up the Meditation.

Meditation is my safety blanket.

Dylan Oliver

Mr Tambourine Man – Bob Dylan

ⓘ

Dylan Oliver arrived on 24th August 2008. My beautiful boy. He was late and so I had to be taken into Kettering General Hospital to be induced.

My God, Rob and I had no idea what to expect! Rob left that evening and I was looking forward to him arriving Sunday morning with the papers. As we had always done, read the papers and taken it *'Easy Like a Sunday Morning…'*

Rob arrived, and I was already in the early stages of labour. At 3:35pm, Dylan was born. Rob and Mum were with me in the delivery suite. He was adorable, but it was also a little bit scary, as the responsibility was huge. I struggled to sleep and switch off after Dylan was born and I felt the anxiety return. I felt vulnerable and a million miles away from my mum and any support. Mum did her best and travelled to Corby on a regular basis, but it was difficult to leave Derrick alone after his stroke. Dylan and I were constantly in the car travelling up and down the M1.

Dylan was and still is beautiful, but he did not like to sleep, and I spent the first three years of his life in a constant sleep-deprived state. I remember watching President Obama win the US election through the night, as I sat with Dylan in the early hours.

After Dylan was born, finding work to fit around childcare was the most impossible task ever. I did a stint working in a *freakin'* Sponge Factory in the evenings. After Rob came home, I would hand over baby Dylan and go off to work in the factory, packing sponges. I was working a night shift in a bloody sponge factory just to pay the bills. It was probably the worst job of my life. I cried and then I left.

-

What followed was a whole heap of sleepless and penniless nights. We were so broke, it was ridiculous.

We had a mortgage and the company were unwilling to have any flexibility or negotiations or leniency when we were unable to make the payments on our small wage. We were at the mercy of the country's economic downturn; our monthly payments went thought the roof!

We finally couldn't take anymore, well mainly me, I think Rob wanted to stay. I was at a very low point in my life. We handed the keys over, packed up and moved back to Dunstable.

We crash landed on our arses, in a rental property in a dodgy area. So, from our beautiful new build family home, we were now paying someone else's mortgage and had a mountain of debts. Losing our house was a hugely emotional and difficult time in our lives. We felt like failures. We felt like our stability had all gone. Our roots had been pulled from the ground. We felt broken, but we supported each other wholeheartedly through it. Yes, we had some rows, but nothing ever broke us. It only made us grow together even stronger.

Rob and I had something special and we would not let life break us. We had our little triangle with Dylan and together we had strength.

No Fixed Abode

Struggle – Tinush featuring Aretha Franklin
ⓘ

Next, I worked for a Housing Authority. It was ironic really, how we were moving from house to house and I was having to deal with queries all day regarding other people's housing options… Knowing that at that time there were no options open for us.

This was a good company, but after 3 months it was clear I had learnt the role, and there were no further opportunities for me to develop.

I was working full time and Dylan was only 3 and had just started at nursery. The company stated that they were flexible, but not willing to be flexible for me. I needed to change my hours as working full time was not helping family life. After a big long battle with the managers, I guess HR stepped in and finally, a job share was granted.

This did help with the boredom for a short while, but not for long. For three days a week I sat in a chair repeating the same advice and processing the same paperwork. In the end I was granted permission to work on a project and I ended up implementing a Social Media platform and creating a policy that went along with it. But my efforts were just sucked up and the work I'd done, along with my initiative were unrecognised and I felt very much unappreciated.

Our house was the first of many rentals; we moved about 6 times in the next 5 years after we left Corby. They were short term, inappropriate properties with high rents. I was never able to relax and feel as though we were at home. We were always packing boxes and moving again. I felt dizzy and unsettled.

There was much confusion and an inability to get our life in order. There was no schedule or structure as we were always living in someone else's house, with their structure and organisation already in place.

At that time, I would always have this feeling that all my belongings were up in the air. I was unable to grow roots and really settle.

Living in rental accommodation, is so nerve-wracking, as you never know when the Landlord or Homeowner is going to pull the rug from under your feet. You never know when you're going to be told, they want to sell or move back in. At any moment, you can be told the rent is going up; all of these aspects are simmering in the background. They had no interest in the upkeep of the house and trying to get any repairs done was a very tough job; if the rent was coming in each month, that was all the landlord cared about.

We also had the constant worry of whether we would pass the initial credit check, with the mountain of debts we had in our name, following us around like a tight scarf around our necks. Panic, plenty of panic and anxiety on top of an already stressful situation of moving home.

During this period of time, I had the following message from Sir Arthur Conan Doyle...

"My Dear along the way, you will experience times of hardship and difficulties. You will wonder why it seems to be constant on occasions. You will doubt your actions and reactions and question your thought process. My Dear you must have faith in the knowledge and wisdom that we bestow upon you.

For as long as you follow the guidance, we provide for you, with love in our hearts at all times you will not go wrong.

Sometimes we step back slightly as you have your own road to travel and lessons to learn, all of which will gift you with knowledge for your soul.

However, always we journey along with you, and protect you with love. You are never alone. Each step that you take is paved with magic, indescribable to many."

Finally, after much fighting and determination and several degrading meetings with the Council. I was able to enter the bidding system for a Council house. I needed some stability and a home that we could finally settle in again. I was placed on the waiting list. I began to bid on properties and soon realised that we had *Bob Hope and No Hope*. We were so far down the priority listing that it would take a lifetime to even get anywhere near an offer.

I wrote to our local MP, we were in an unfortunate situation, whereby we were overlooked by the system. Rob was working and earning just over the threshold, neither of us were on benefits therefore, not entitled to any help. Rob literally earned a little over the threshold and it left us in no-man's land. I continued to write to the MP and explained this, along with our background. Finally, he helped us, and we were moved up the bidding list. It changed our life and we are eternally grateful.

The bidding system was like a lottery. Every two weeks the Council would open up a new bidding cycle. Initially, we were banded in D, which basically means you have no *freakin'* chance of even getting close to a suitable property.

Thankfully the MP changed this, and we were then promoted to Band B. This was a game changer. So, when bidding opened at midnight, I would sadly be awake at this time, trying to get my bid in before any other equally desperate families did the same. You'd have to wait until bidding closed to find out where you were placed. If by any Grace of God, you were top three, there was real hope.

I couldn't believe it the day I was told we had won the bidding. We had finally secured a house.

This phase has only made me more determined.

During a Spiritual Development Workshop, I was told that I will have my Castle again and this is what I continuously strive for. A home to call our own again. Right now, our Housing Association house is beautiful, but very, very small. We have all our old furniture from our old own home, so nothing fits. In reality, I don't want a Castle, all I hope for is a space to breathe and write and a good size garden for a 'Man Cave' for Rob and goal posts for Dylan.

A Decade
English Rose – The Jam

The ten years that took me from 30 to 40, were not easy years. A test of character and strength is an understatement. It's no wonder there were moments of extreme weakness and an inability to function or focus.

For sure my resilience pulled me through, there was no other option but on reflection, I felt as though I was wading through quicksand.

Now as I emerge on the other side. I look towards this next decade with a sense of calmness and contentment. As a family we have made it and now we can begin to enjoy a life that we wanted, that we have fought so hard to create. At last we have solid foundations to build upon for our future. A future as a family, with love at the core. For this is the core that held us so tight, when we needed so much more.

I appreciate all that we have and gratefully feel blessed. It's been a test of endurance, of which I have gained. My strength and courage can now take a rest, there is no need to keep fighting, this is my place of comfort and rest.

A ten-year cycle has gone full circle.

SEEKING

We are free to exercise our creativity. It is a great time to establish a true communication channel with our own Spirit.

My Spirit Guide - Red Mountain
A Horse with No Name - America
ⓘ

When it comes to hearing voices, there are several different types of voices and entities that can be communicating with us and there are different reasons for hearing these voices. The voices that children hear are most often the voices of their Spirit Guides or Angels who are part of their guidance system.

We are never alone. We are born with a group of Spirit Guides whose job it is to keep us safe throughout this lifetime, and to guide us to carry out our mission and purpose on Earth, if we are willing to listen and follow them.

Our guides will continue to communicate with us, but their voices may become silent over time because of our fear, doubt or resistance, which makes it frustrating for them to communicate with us, and for us to understand them. They will then communicate with us in our dreams or through various signs and synchronicities, which takes a great deal of energy on their behalf. Our Guides and Angels often communicate messages to guide us to safety and happiness, which will give us the feeling of being urged, prompted, pushed or even compelled, but always in a loving and caring way.

-

I met my Guide during a Guided Meditation in my late 20's in with a development group.

He came to me with strength. In my third eye I could see he was bare chested, very tall and he was wearing a long piece of silver and topaz jewellery as a necklace. He had a brown leather bag hung across his chest.

His hair was long, straight, and dark. I clearly remember seeing that his nose was prominent with a slightly raised bridge. He was very tall and had large rough hands. He wore a short cloth to cover his modesty and long calf length boots. The name I was given was Red Mountain.

At that stage I felt blessed to have met him. He had a gentle but assertive energy about him. There was power but in a very calm way. I was not scared or afraid and I felt very excited to have actually met and connected with my Guide. It was a very big moment in my journey. From this moment I knew things were going to be different.

I had begun to meditate regularly, and I was already connecting with my Guardian Angels during Meditation. So, I guess my mind was more receptive and I believe that Spirit was recognising that the time was right for me to once again develop further.

-

Throughout my life, I have been given the space to absorb each level of development, before being guided on to the next level. Like a phased journey – with time to understand and embrace each step.

Red Mountain was my Guide and advisor and I felt safe in his guidance. I was dedicated to meditating every day. If I didn't, I became cranky; I just knew it was something I needed to do.

To record my journey, I started to keep journals as I had done when I was a teenager. I would detail things I had seen during my Meditations, any signs and symbols or messages I was receiving for myself or other people.

Spotting little white feathers was becoming an everyday occurrence. A little white feather showing up in an unexpected place is a sign from the Angels that they are with us. Because of the sheer number of feathers, I felt compelled to read the book 'Angels in my Hair' by Lorna Byrne. This book is a great insight into how the Angels work and support us in everyday life; as experienced by Lorna during her very testing and difficult life.

I went for a reading with a respected local Medium. I'd seen her before with Mum. Only this time when I went to her, she told me that I was a Medium and I was capable of doing the same work as her. She told me that she was being guided to take me under her wing and teach me how to become a Medium.

This was absolutely amazing, and I was floating on air, the excitement at knowing that there was someone else who knew what I knew, and she was willing to help me get to where I needed to be. I went back to my Mum's and I was full of emotion. I felt tearful because my journey of development meant so much to me.

She and I arranged to meet a few days later, she would collect me and take me to an event that she was involved in and I would observe and do readings with her. The night she collected me, was a dark cold December evening. I was super excited but also super stressed.

Dylan wasn't very well, and Rob was coming down with it too. I felt so torn, do I leave Rob and Dylan at home? I couldn't cancel, what if this was my only chance?

It didn't go to plan and Rob urgently called me home. Now I felt terrible; embarrassed and upset. In fact, I was mortified. I got home to a house of germs and felt like my only opportunity had been stopped before it had even started.

Now in reflection, I firmly believe this wasn't actually the right path for me.

My heart and soul are in writing and teaching; in helping other people to find their own direction and develop their own intuition and gift. I am supposed to be sharing the philosophies from the Spirit World not giving messages from loved ones so much. Not that that never happens, but it isn't where my main focus lies.

My journals were becoming more about the wisdom I was receiving from Red Mountain. I was working at the Housing Association at this time, really struggling during the day but getting great comfort from Spirit as I would write at night and Meditate in the morning before work.

There was something about the sound of a super sharp pencil on paper, this would help me to absorb myself even more in what I was hearing from Spirit. I would capture all that I was being told, these messages didn't come to me at all throughout the day, it would only be when I was in my Meditation Room, candles lit, and intention and focus was with Spirit.

When I share that I am a Medium, people will often ask me if I have anything for them – any messages? But for me it isn't like that – I have to be in the right 'Zone'. It's also about respect, I don't like to just assume that Spirit will give me information willy-nilly – without setting the intention correctly. I feel as though I owe them the honour of connecting in a certain way and following the rituals I have in place.

I guess since being a young child, I have always felt as though it was something very special and it has always felt very personal to me. I didn't really share it with many people, other than my Mum. I would read to her paragraphs that I had been given. I always felt safe in trusting my Mum. She would be happy for me that I was receiving such confirmation and in excitement, as my connection to Spirit deepened. Occasionally I would share something with Rob, but not everything.

It has always been quite a solitude journey, as I wasn't looking to anyone else for confirmation or interest. The messages were very personal to me and my journey, and I didn't need or want to allow in any doubt from others, because I was sure about what I was receiving and my certainty was unwavering.

Red Mountain is always with me, whether I am happy or sad. The problem is sometimes when I have been super sad, I have lost my way and have not connected as often as I should. I have sometimes stepped away from listening and following guidance. Only when I begin to listen again – do things get back on track. They have guided me in times of uncertainty.

That feeling of faith that I get from Spirit is invaluable. They are able to alleviate many doubts and fears – and that knowingness is indescribably comforting. So often I have felt the soothing arms of Spirit (metaphorically speaking) around me, and just know that it was all going to be okay. With this knowledge I am able to pass on security to Rob and family.

Red Mountain has given me more information about him and his life. I wasn't really interested in history at school and don't really remember information about the civil war or anything — however, Red Mountain has taught me so much.

Red Mountain...

"I am a Navajo Indian Chief. I lived in the same time as the Civil War. I have always been your guide since birth - I used to talk to you as a child - you were aware of the chatter, but you were unaware that you had the gift and you were scared to see anything. I have always held back until you were ready and now you are ready - but still you hear more than you see. We are working with you and people will come to you knowing that you are a wise one with lots to share and give. I love you Child of the Universe I am always with you."

"My People...

A golden sun glows brightly as it lowers its energies and gives in to the shadows of the evening. My people gather as we have always done, we come together to join as one.

We respect the entities of each of our brothers, connecting on a level of deep understanding and trust. A bond unbroken by time or generations. A chord that will tie us forever more.

This land that we have walked, this land has carried us and we obey the laws. Our heaven is this very land - and we have fought hard with the men who have endeavoured to move us away from our sacred space.

For my People, as time changes our paths, the constant breath that whispers through our connected souls will remain unchanged.

People of the forgotten land, may you embrace all that is bestowed upon you, your Spirit shall never dampen, and your eternal flame will never falter.

This world will constantly battle the elements and anger with deceit not far behind. Many will experience hardship; breath deep and trust your inner chord - this will carry you through."

A little more about him…

"Tall and strong, a man of his word. I give you nothing more than the wisdom within me. I will carry you along your journey.

I died a young man, but an old soul. Gunshot killed me in the end. A war over land with an army."

On the 11th August 2013 he told me…

"It is a big world out there and you are entitled to your chunk of experiences that will help you grow and allow you to continue down your destined path. Travel is a necessity for you, it is not just a luxury, it will help you to grow and nourish your soul. Please see it as your entitlement and allow yourself to dream of travel and distant places. There are religions for you to explore and cultures for you to live, this will help you to work out, who you are, and what are your own beliefs, not the limiting beliefs, which you have inherited. My Child you are free to roam.

Do not fear about finances to fund these explorations, for this will happen, more financial gain is coming your way, and you will free up time to be able to explore. It is time to believe that abundance is rightly yours, it is not selfish or greedy, it is needed to help you grow.

Listen to the ideas that pop into your head, you have so many. The money will come along to help you. Once you are free the creativity will flow. Allow this to happen there are no limitations.

Have faith My Child, you are a Child of the Universe. You are beautiful. This is an amazing chapter of your life. You will look back and create a book from your journey and people will read it."

After writing a piece that had left me feeling a little overwhelmed, I went out for a little fresh air and took a detour, ending up in a little shop getting a message from a Medium; asking me, "When are you going to release this book?" She told me to write in nature and surround myself with dogs. My Dad now lives in France, rescuing dogs, with his own forest!

She only confirmed to me what Red Mountain had already been telling me. Red Mountain had told me that I have to immerse myself in nature, this is true, I know it helps my creativity and wellbeing. Recently I have been asking him to guide me once again, as I didn't know how to present this book or even what I should do with it once I had completed it. So, I have thrown it to him and allowed him to sort it for me. As I write this now, he is with me from meditation this morning, we are still working together. So rather than forcing the issue I will allow it to flow free, like life itself. It's in your hands Red Mountain.

A Warning…

"Remember it will not always be easy. Some days you will have doubts that will hinder your progress. This will challenge you're staying power and ability to believe in yourself.

My Child you may experience and feel the emotions of others closely connected to you and the damage experienced, through the traumas of life. What you must remember is, that other people's traumas are affecting your ability to move on with your life. It is nothing intentional or of malice. My Child it is a deep-rooted conditioning that has controlled their life and it threatens to control your existence.

My Child you will need to step back and ascertain your own rightful and courageous independence.

You have your own story to write, you are not a consequence of someone else's story.

Protect yourself as unintentionally there is a drain on your energy.

Allow yourself to become the Master of your own destiny.

As you approach your 40's your wisdom grows. You will need to stand in your own shadow and not that of another. No need to challenge - no need to be right. Let it pass and follow your own destiny.

I will always guide you - look to no other than your own inner soul and wisdom."

Route 66
Long Train Running – The Doobie Brothers

It was October 2013 and I was at my friend Lisa's house for our regular, Thursday night. Girls' night. I got a call from Dad. I fell silent; I hadn't expected him to deliver the news that his partner of 20 years had died suddenly. I did not know what to say, I had to process this information; I simply said, "Dad, I'll phone you back."

I soon learnt that Dad had found Chris when he had returned from work. He had tried to resuscitate her, but it was too late.

I left for Cornwall the very next day. It was the longest train journey I had ever done. I took a train into London and changed for Exeter. That part was pretty standard. It was when I got to Exeter that it all got a little strange. Next, I boarded a rickety old wooden train from Exeter which terminated in Bideford. And that was the end of the line. Next, I had to take a £100 taxi ride from Bideford to Kilkhampton. I arrived at Dad's exhausted, but happy to be there to comfort him as best as I could.

I knew very little about my Dad and his partner's life as I had not ever been too involved. They had been very heavily into Carriage Driving and had been quite successful; competing in competitions at Windsor and against Prince Philip. I went along once and happened to be standing shoulder to shoulder with HRH The Queen, as she watched Prince Philip. I tried to get involved in this life that they lead, but it was like another 'square peg – round hole' situation. She was so focussed on the horses, and Dad worked all hours to fund their dream.

When I arrived at Dad's, the house felt so odd. It was as though time had stood still. I stayed for a few days, made calls for Dad and dealt with the Coroner. Then left to go back home again, and did the same journey, back and forth a few more times.

Myself, Rob and Dylan went back for the funeral. The funeral was held in Bodmin and the view from the Crematorium was amazing. We entered as a unit. Me, Dad, my stepbrother and sister, but we left broken.

After the funeral, we walked out to look at the flowers. I was left standing totally alone. Rob and Dylan hadn't come to the cremation as Dylan was only 3. My Dad mingled, and I stood there like that round peg in a square hole; I didn't know a soul.

I supported my Dad, as best as I could through this time, but his sadness was enormous, we spoke every day on the phone for the next year.

I was given messages from Spirit for Dad from his partner; apologising for certain things, she spoke about candle wax. This was particularly relevant as he had been cleaning candle wax off of the fireplace the night before, whilst thinking about her. At the time of receiving the message I thought, 'I can't pass this on to Dad', I had absolutely no idea how candle wax would be relevant to Dad, but amazingly, it was indeed very relevant, more than I could have imagined. I'm glad I overcame my initial hesitance to share that message.

On the day that she had passed over, I remember going for a walk at lunchtime and noticing a little Robin. The robin was making himself quite obvious, not shying away from me. It is said that a Robin is a sign of Spirit being close to you. I spent some time watching the Robin on that day, wondering what the message was. That evening I found out.

As part of my Dad's grieving process he took a trip to America, to travel Route 66 with his friend. Without a shadow of a doubt I believe this was the best thing he could have done, it enabled him to move forward again with his life and to remember who he was.

Whilst he was away, he visited New Mexico, and the Red Mountain area and whilst he was there, he visited a shop run by Navajo's; Native Americans. Dad decided to buy a necklace for me, a silver and turquoise necklace. Amazingly this necklace was very similar to the necklace worn by my guide Red Mountain when he had first visited me in meditation.

In the shop, which was run by a Navajo lady, he asked for some help as he was looking for something for his daughter. The lady didn't say too much, she just picked up the necklace and put it in his hand, saying "I think she would like this."

He remembers that at the time it seemed a little odd (his words – not mine). It felt as though the whole decision was taken out of his hands, and very quickly and promptly he was given this necklace, that was to be such a poignant part of my journey.

I find this outstanding. It confirmed a lot to me and to this day, I continue to be in awe at the way Spirit work.

This story was also featured in a national magazine; Spirit & Destiny.

Dowsing

Blow Your Mind - Jamiroquai

ⓓ

The pendulum is a powerful tool that receives information from the vibrations and energy waves emitted by people, places, thoughts and things; the energy that you cannot see.

Albert Einstein was known to perform impressive feats with such dowsing tools. He believed that it was powered by electromagnetism: very similar to the birds that migrate following the Earth's magnetic field, dowsers react to energies that are unseen, still to this day, it is not fully understood.

It is said that the pendulum creates a bridge for the gap between the logical mind and the intuitive mind. Many use the pendulum to connect to a higher source; this process is called divining, as the information and answers received are believed to come from a divine source. Research and evidence from many scientists indicate that the pendulum responds to electromagnetic energy that radiates from everything on Earth.

No one knows for sure how the pendulum works, but the important thing is that it does work! Other famous dowsing advocates in history include Leonardo Da Vinci (inventor), Robert Boyle (father of modern chemistry), Charles Richet (Nobel Prize winner), and General Patton (U.S. Army). So, its use is not to be sniffed at. If it's good enough for Albert Einstein, then it is good enough for me.

I went to a workshop in Leighton Buzzard. It was a beautiful evening and I learnt so much. I was instructed to choose my first pendulum and I did. I chose a fairly simple one, nothing too fancy. It was a pyramid shape and hung from a long silver chain with a pearl on the end.

We were taught how to ask the pendulum questions and watch for how it gives its answers. I was told to ask whether my name was Nicola and to see which direction the pendulum swung in. A yes was given, and it circled clockwise. I was told next to find out how it would swing for the answer 'No'. So, I asked the pendulum a clear question that would give a 'No answer'; something like did I have blonde hair. The pendulum swung from left to right. And it is that simple.

So, we worked that evening finding out more about our Soul Ages. We learnt more about our passed lives and generally connected with our Pendulum, learning to trust the answers that were given.

Soon after, my Dad asked me for some help, a dog in Spain had gone missing from the Rescue Centre. I used a map of the area and began to dowse over the area. I sliced up the map and worked over each section. Asking if the dog was in this area and receiving a yes or no answer.

Eventually I managed to pin down the exact area that the dog had been last seen but annoyingly not the area it was to be found, as the dog kept wandering and I was unable to pinpoint its position. The lady in Spain was shocked that I'd tracked down the exact site the dog had gone missing from. Psychic work and Spirituality hold no boundaries and can work across the globe.

Many people are still insistent on sitting down with a medium or a psychic for a face to face reading, when actually it doesn't matter where in the world you, or they are.

One Very Lucky Cat
Chasing Pavements - Adele

ⓘ

There was a time when Red Mountain helped us find our cat, Purdy. It was a lovely warm Summer afternoon. We had a knock on our door from a neighbour, she was asking if we had a black and white cat. Her daughter had just seen a cat get run over by a taxi and flipped up in the air.

Usually Purdy would be somewhere close to the house, but on this occasion, she was nowhere to be found. We became quite frantic searching for her and realised the longer we were unable to find her the more obvious it seemed that it was Purdy that had been hit by the taxi.

The hours passed, and it turned to night time, and she was still nowhere to be found. At this stage I decided to turn to Spirit for help. So firstly, I began to use my pendulum for answers, but I guess because I was too frantic, I wasn't asking clear enough questions. The pendulum and I were not connected on this occasion.

So, I turned to Red Mountain. I tuned in through Meditation and connected. He said the following words to me "She is one lucky cat." He told me that she was still alive, and he told me where to find her. I told Rob and he went out to find her, turning left out of the house and going up to the top of the road. He heard a little "meow" and Purdy came out from a bush. She had a bloody nose and seemed shaken. We phoned the vets, and they prepared for the worst after we had told them she had been hit by a taxi. We took her to the vets and they confirmed that she was one lucky cat, with no serious injuries.

Since then she has been the same happy cat, only a little more careful around traffic.

Fall Out

Smoke on the Water – Deep Purple

"My Child sometimes in life people will let you down. You cannot control this and nor should you. Everyone has their lessons to learn, sometimes they can be painful and sometimes they may hurt deeply. Again this will only test and question your faith and knowing - that there is a place far unreachable.

As you progress your skin will toughen, but your heart will always remain the same. Only with a tougher exterior. You will only let a few break through, and you will not experience a hurt like this again. You have overcome a hurt that was simmering since childhood.

It had to come to the surface to give you freedom and allow you to break the chord. You are free now to be the flower and light within – let your true self shine.

You are over the pain, it is time to allow your Spirit to settle into a new rhythm. Allow him to live his own lessons. Again you cannot control his lessons, and nor can you control the lessons of others.

This experience will free you from a lifetime of confusion and bring about a clarity that will guide you into a maturity of consciousness. Blessed be oh sweet one, lessons learnt, now be free, a time of harmony, will now follow thee."

-Red Mountain

How did my Spirituality Develop?

A Change is Gonna Come – Aretha Franklin

ⓘ

Red Mountain….

"The divine, the power within, a force so strong and unexpecting, only those of a certain understanding will ever flourish as the source intended.

It is a task of oneness and a task not to be taken lightly. For those that have been selected, will truly master all of the source within them.

You My Child are one of the very few, who have followed this inner wisdom, and allowed yourself to step along the lines of those created for you by the master beings of previous existence.

As you so do. With all that you encounter. Such a generosity of Spirit is so seldom felt, as that, that resides within you.

As you continue to work with Spirit at the source, your heart will open like a summer flower. A gift so raw, a beauty so bespoke, a tenderness so sweet – all so unique."

*"For it is not your Gift alone,
it is a Gift to be shared."*

-Red Mountain

"You wonder about your sensitivity, and fear that it is of harm. My Child be rest assured, this only enables you to work on a connection so pure – people will be in awe of your inner wisdom.

No longer, do you wonder where this wisdom is drawn from, no longer do you wonder where your words are channelled from. For no longer do you care – as this wisdom is now a part of you.

A world of infinite resources and connection is at your fingertips. An endless supply of love and opportunities lay ahead for you my Child, as the world begins to respond to you.

Special and unique is all that you are. Our love for you as our Spirit helper is the light around you. Engulfed in energy, you are protected and encouraged.

Keep walking forward, replacing fear with abundant faith. For never more certain, than you are now of correctness and direction. You will be Heaven's helper and shine on in the Angelic light."

-

I started attending a Circle in Leighton Buzzard. It was a lovely circle and the ladies who ran it were very welcoming and friendly. We started off by Meditating and discussing what we saw, what we experienced and sharing any messages we felt we had. We then went on to reading cards for each other and throughout the weeks we moved on to reading ribbons and candle wax and other psychic tools.

I also met here the Author that had written the Doris Stokes books. Doris Stokes was a famous Medium. Her book published in 1980, Voices in My Ear: The Autobiography of a Medium was quite significant in my journey. I liked the way that she worked; it was none of the traditional stage medium stuff or spooky séance stuff. She was 'Down to Earth', and I liked her.

Another book that inspired me was The Silver Birch books. These were books about conversations with a Spirit Guide called Silver Birch and channelled by a Medium.

One evening stands out in my memory. At Circle, during Meditation, I experienced something quite different and very deep. As I was in Meditation, I saw a gravestone and the markings said… 'Here lies Sir Arthur Conan Doyle Born 1860.' At the same time, I was aware of the smell of cigar smoke in the room. We continued to Meditate and when I came around, I was feeling very light and energised. Something had just happened, and I knew it had made a big difference to my journey.

I had not really smelt the cigar smoke before, the only smell I had experienced before was from my friend, that had passed. The cigar smoke I believe was an extra nudge, as I had possibly been ignoring Sir Arthur's previous attempts at getting my attention. This smell really made me sit up and listen. I have not smelt it really since then, as I now have a direct link. He often reminds me he is not psychic, and I am not to ask him if it might rain today. He is there for my Spiritual development and writing only.

When I got home that evening after circle, I was buzzing. I *Googled* Sir Arthur and was shocked to discover that he was instrumental in the setup of the Spiritualist National Union Church and also had big interest in the Arthur Findlay College of Psychic Studies. I also discovered that he was born in May 1859. So, I was a few months out with 1860.

Another *Googling* session also told me that he was one of the first people to drive a motor car. This was no surprise to me as he had already told me about his excitement at driving a car.

I didn't realise at the time the impact or hugeness of this connection to Sir Arthur. I was overwhelmed but also pretty cool about it. The more that I was developing, the less things began to surprise me. It appeared some experiences were just meant to be, and I didn't always know what it would mean at the time.

It felt quite special to have such a connection with a Spiritual Ambassador and I guess it must have meant that I was to be a good Ambassador for Spirit if he was choosing to work with me. I definitely felt honoured and I wasn't going to waste this opportunity. I needed to make the most of it.

After this, I knew I needed to start to focus on writing, with the encouragement and coaching from none other than one of the greatest writers of our time, it was nothing I should ignore.

Being guided by Sir Arthur, I ended up talking to another medium and writer; we chatted and messaged each other for a while. After talking for a short while we quickly discovered that Sir Arthur also guided her. She went on to tell me that I reminded Sir Arthur of one of his daughters, and this is part of his reason for working with me.

This was a monumental part of my journey because where he led me next was to my next circle and to my next teacher. Coincidentally I became very aware that my new teacher was guided by Gordon Higginson, a great companion of Sir Arthur as they supported each other in the quest to pioneer the Spiritualist College Arthur Findlay.

So, it would seem that Sir Arthur was starting to introduce me to people that were right for me and would support me in developing and deepening my understanding of Mediumship.

I began attending the new circle, travelling a good 45 minutes down the M1. I didn't care though; I was prepared to give that extra effort for my dedication to my development. Immediately it felt as though I was being stretched appropriately. I had respectfully outgrown the psychic circles and needed to focus on my Mediumship and my connection to Spirit.

It was time for me to strengthen my connection and build on my confidence.

At weekends I would leave Rob and Dylan to fend for themselves whilst I went on another Spiritual Development workshop, now I was standing in front of the group and delivering messages. I was beginning to trust and deliver the messages I was receiving. I was working for Spirit and I loved the energy that came with it.

I spent every Sunday for a month travelling down the M1 to learn Tarot with a teacher form the London School of Psychic Studies. This was hugely enjoyable and if I'm honest, quite tiring; working all week then committing to Tarot on the weekend.

When working psychically, the energy is heavy for me. You are working from the energy of the person you are reading. It can be very draining. When you are working with Spirit the energy is lighter and less draining.

I began to develop further and comfortably moved on to trance Mediumship. This flowed easily working with my guide Red Mountain.

My teacher arranged for me to go out with her to a local SNU (Spiritualist National Union) church working with her as Fledglings, to give messages to the church in order to practice their skills. I sat up on the stage in a row of 6 other Fledglings. I was not comfortable. I felt so out of my depth it was painful. What bothered me so much was that the other readers had a certain style about their readings. They had that tried and tested-stage-medium style and that just wasn't me. I couldn't use those cliché lines or style of delivery. I knew that's what the audience wanted and I just couldn't do it. It confirmed to me that I don't work like many mediums, and its best I use my own style, and not try to copy the style of others. I cannot and will not be something I am not.

Red Mountain said to me...

"Never doubt that the knowledge we send you is incorrect, sometimes it is your translation of the message that may be incorrect. This will come with practice. Do not be disheartened when you appear to be wrong, this will only make you work harder.

You are a very clever girl, and always have been. The way that you think about things deeply and question situations.

Your mind will spin with possibilities and ideas. This way of thinking will pave the way for you and your family."

Connection

Stairway to Heaven – Led Zeppelin
ⓘ

So, I think what surprised me the most, when I began to receive messages, was that it was so easy, and I had probably been hearing Spirit long before I actually defined it as Mediumship.

You see, it is not some booming godly voice that gives me the messages. It is much subtler than that and sounds just like my own voice.

How I know when this is Spirit and my Spirit Guides is that I will often hear things I didn't know and had no way of knowing. I will often hear terms, mannerisms and phrases that I would not normally use; sometimes I do not know the meaning of the words I am hearing. The voices of Guides and Spirit will always be loving and encouraging; any voice that is critical, nasty, judgmental or mean is not a voice of your Guides.

If anything, it is probably your critical voice or self-talk, which would need addressing with Mindfulness. As this critical self- talk can be debilitating.

Red Mountain…

"We are here – simply as we are, to absorb the world and all of the goings on.

We are here to ponder about the life that is beyond these earthly boundaries.

For what exists beyond, is a world of beauty and a trouble-free world where pain is a distant memory. There is no more of the difficulties that once were – when you travelled in your earthly body.

There is no more, of the doubts and fears you once encountered. For these are the very lessons that brought you to a place of harmony and peace. It is a lovely place, when you are working on a higher vibration. A vibration that is not inhibited by many others – the space is infinite.

You will be living the life that you have been preparing for."

Now my connection to Red Mountain is instant. Although most of the time I prefer to go to a quiet place so that I can concentrate and know that it is him I am hearing.

Initially, if I wanted to connect to Spirit I would start by Meditating. I would go into a Meditation, ensuring that I would be left in peace and not disturbed for a while. Preferably sitting, so that I wouldn't be at risk of falling asleep.

I would visualise myself clearing each of my Chakras.

I would visualise a beautiful white light surrounding each individual Chakra with the white light rising to the Spirit world. I would continue this visualisation moving through the Crown, Third Eye, Throat, Heart, Solar Plexus, Sacral and finally my Root Chakra, with my entire body surrounded in white light as it is extending out to the universe - I and the Spirit world merge and our energies become one.

Next, I would call in my Spirit Guides and Helpers for protection, calling always on Archangel Michael and Red

Mountain. I would ask them to join me in this ball of pure white light. Then I would visualise the ball of white light growing bigger and bigger as it grows in energy.

I would take Red Mountain's hand and we would begin the walk up a very long staircase, plain in colour, just big stone steps. We would walk side by side until we reached a huge door with a big round brass door handle. I would turn the handle, to open the door, to a room filled with nothing, nothing but a large cream sheepskin rug.

I would take a seat on the rug with Red Mountain; sometimes he would give me some healing, other times we would just sit.

From a door in the corner of the room I would set the intention, that if anyone in Spirit wishes to come forward and give any messages I was open to receive.

This was Spirits' opportunity to come forward with any messages. Or it was a time for Red Mountain and I to sit and for him to share his wisdom with me and I would begin to write to capture his wisdom and messages.

Red Mountain…

"You are your own power – your own source. There is nothing more that you would need – all that you need is within you. Look no further, seek no more, allow and you will see, just what you are capable of.

Heaven is all around you – feel its familiarity, for once again you can be sure that your existence is that of eternal knowing.

You shall never be alone, for even if you are feeling uncertain of your bonds, and at times you will. Know always that you are protected and cherished."

Messages Received
Message in a Bottle – The Police

There have been moments in my development when I have been curious to learn more about some of the big things in life. I have pondered on questions and wanted to know what Spirits perspective is on certain things…

I have a direct link to a Greater Source and an inquisitive mind, so why not ask questions?

My Questions to Red Mountain…
Q: Tell me about Love?
A: *"Love is the most heavenly emotion that you will experience, whilst in your earthly body. This pure love travels straight from the core of all creativity. There is nothing purer and nothing sweeter than the love shared by human beings. Love begins from that very first moment a sparkle of dust is considered in the solar system. It is shared as the most optimum treasure that a man can give. To be loved and to love is pure and eternal in the ethereal."*

Q: Tell Me about Passing Over?
"When a man passes from our world and emerges into yours, we are sad, and you rejoice. When a man passes from your world and re-enters our world we celebrate - our brother has returned.

It's a constant see-saw of our universes balancing out the kinship for the brother. His Spirit will always live on, a light forever bright. Know that the Spirit is eternal."

Q: I asked Sir Arthur Conan Doyle, why do I have this gift?

SA: "You have this gift because you have a special connection with Spirit and have done since you were a child; you are a wise soul and a gentle character the perfect combination for a learner and a teacher. We are working with you because you are connected by soul group and we know that you have an open mind. You have lived a chequered life and have life experience. Which has not left you wounded but has left you enlightened. You have the ability to connect on all levels - but you must also learn to disconnect. You must also work on an earthly level and not always on a Spiritual Level. You will learn - you are getting there. The teaching you are doing is all part of your Spiritual journey."

This message from Sir Arthur Conan Doyle reminded me that I do need to be careful not to allow all my energies to be drained. I am an Empath and can become very tired when I am working with people. This is a good reminder to take time for myself as I do need to cleanse my soul regularly.

Red Mountain said…

"I am with you My Child, no need to connect further, my connection to you is quicker and not so long winded."

Red Mountain is reassuring me here that he is always with me, and whereas before I would do a lengthy meditation to speak with him – it was now unnecessary to make it so long winded!! Even he is a simple 'Down to Earth' man.

I was feeling quite disconnected at a certain point in my life, I felt as though I wasn't able to connect properly, and I was feeling quite disillusioned and my faith was being questioned. I turned to Spirit for some reassurance. And to show some frustration towards them.

Q: What has been happening - why has my faith been so challenging?
A: *"We do not have all the answers and there is much for you to learn by yourself. If we were to path your way with certainty - what would you learn and how would your Spirit grow? Do not allow doubts to block your connection as we will never leave your side, only we will step back and hold out our arms, as there are times when certainly you will fall. These falls and bruises only go on to shape your soul's maturity. The more that you curse us (as we know that you do!) the more that we hear your frustrations with us*
- the more that we know you are learning."

Q: Why have you given me wrong information?
A: *"As Spirit Guides and helpers we are here to support you, although, please remember that we are not psychics, you must use your own intuition for these answers. We can only guide you as to what is right for your soul. Think about the way that you ask your questions, we will answer exactly what we have been asked. If this is incorrect this is your responsibility."*

Q: Where will my work take me?
A: *"You have recently blocked and this has created insecurity on your behalf. Allow us in again and we will guide you along with the Angels, this will create opportunities. You must give your permission for us to work for you and watch as it all unfolds. Step back in faith."*

Thoughts on Daily Mindfulness

"As you go about your daily routine, ask yourself what can I do differently today? Why must most days mirror that of the day before? Each day we must challenge ourselves to go about our "routine" in a different way. This situation which we refer to as "comfort zone" maybe preventing you from living the life or being, the being that you could be. Be Bold. Be Brave for you can make a difference, dare yourself to think and look at things differently. Look for the miracle in each day."

Caution…

"You cannot control others; let them be. They are on their own journey – you cannot sway them you must accept others for who they are. We are with you always to help you and you have been learning some important lessons.

Be careful, who you trust, not all are as they seem.

Accept others for who they are.

Keep interested in your own being – Mind, Body & Soul.

Learn to take criticism.

Relax and have fun.

Be organised.

I love you My Child and will always be here. Don't be critical of yourself everyone is learning, and you are lucky that you are open to learning and change."

Messages Given

Redemption Song – Bob Marley

ⓓ

Red Mountain says…

"Sometimes you find it had to connect, as you are quite simple in your approach, remember I keep telling you the connection is there, no need to lengthen the process, it is there, constant like a tap. However, if you wish to connect and give messages from loved ones you will need to go deeper. Prepare to fly My Child, you have access to higher wisdom. Embrace it."

When I am wanting to work with Spirit to gain messages from those that have passed, I go to a different place. I climb the stairs and open the doorway to Spirit.

My friend Lisa came around for me to test my connection and see if I could give her a message. She arrived in a pair of trainers… At that time it was unusual to see her in trainers! This was my first shock as Spirit had told me she would. I went on to connect to her Dad and give her a message that went on to free her from a thousand emotions. I gave her the confirmation it was her Dad by addressing her as he always used to; reassuring her with his words of comfort, often used.

My friend wrote these words to me the day after her message…

"I came home feeling refreshed and very relaxed. By seeing you last night, and connecting to my Dad, him telling me, that he did love me, and he was sorry, and he hadn't meant to leave me – was exactly what I needed to hear. Then you said the immortal line "I was his girl", which he had always said.

You had confirmed that he had been close to me, and I had felt him. You gave me words from him that I have longed to hear since I was 8 years old.

I have had a tough time, and probably will have more, but knowing that my dad has my back, as do you. No words can describe or detail how you have given me my life back."

Confirmation from Red Mountain…
"Yes, My Child you are beginning to recognise and understand your own ability you no longer need the confirmation from others of the correctness of your connection and messages. You are working for and with Spirit. In God's name, we work together to give evidence and proof of Spirit. Your messages will now get stronger and you will begin to build up more of a story and a picture of emotions.

This is another turning point for you as Doris Stokes communicated with her guide… You and I communicate, and it will only get stronger.

Well done for your continued effort and work unselfishly connecting to Spirit we are happy to be working with you."

More Messages given…
I gave a message to dear friend of the family Dani, who was being given a message from an old partner. Even I was

surprised at the information given that I would not have known about, like the accuracy of the details regarding some Green tiles around a fireplace.

Another message for Dani, gave me the feelings of freedom as I connected to her Mother, the inability to tie her Mother down. Her Mother had been ill with Dementia, before she had passed, and it really felt as though she was making up for lost time and lack of movement. She showed me Alpine meadows. What I found beautiful was the feeling and emotions that I felt during the connection. I could really sense the character of her mother. I sensed the inability to want to commit, as she was off living her life again. Numb with Dementia before she passed away and now nothing was going to stop her.

I had initially thought that this reading was a little bit insignificant, but actually it turned out to be very relevant for Dani and she took some comfort from it.

Dani's thoughts on these readings ...

"Having known you since you were about 4yrs old I've watched you grow into a young woman from being a gentle child that fitted in so well amongst adults, in a very subtle way. Almost seen and not heard! You have always been a sensitive person and wise beyond your years but in a soft, unimposing way.

As you have linked into the Spirit world, I personally have seen you grow even more as if you have found your correct path and guidance.

Your messages have proven to be so accurate and stated sayings that would not have been openly said by that passed person, yet you stated them word for word... and what joy you have given by sharing them in a very subtle and caring way, thank you for sharing your gift."

Dani continues to be an inspiration to me as she strives to fulfil her dreams. Dani and I have a shared understanding in our 'Only Child Status', we have an unwritten bond and I value Dani's gentle guidance and mentoring enormously.

-

One day, Dad contacted me to ask for some advice. Dad and his new partner Gloria had sadly and tragically lost one of their dogs in a freaky accident. Dad was asking for any message I could receive. So, I channelled the energy of this beautiful dog. I felt the love and gratitude this dog had for Gloria.

'Mimi' had been a rescue dog. She and Gloria had such a strong bond. I sketched the area that Mimi had been buried and gave Gloria the comfort that she needed to know that Mimi had passed over and was at peace.

When I went to visit Dad for the first time, I showed Dad the sketch I had drawn, and it was identical to the burial patch – facing the forest on the hill next to the allotment. This blew Dad away… and me!

Dad has said that he always knew that I was different, I had always been very focussed. He has said that I was always very mature and that I thought very deeply. Dad says that the readings I have given him have always been very accurate, as though I always seem to just *know*. At times he said my intuition is spooky, as I will call him at the very moment, he has picked up the phone to call me. As though I have a sixth sense and then call him.

-

My cousin and her husband recently lost a friend. She messaged me one morning and asked if I could connect with him. As it was so recent since he had passed I was not expecting to get anything from him. However, he obviously had other ideas and had orchestrated the situation. I sat down with some paper and a pen and began to write his message. He told me that he had been ready to go and had been preparing himself for the cross over. He had known what to expect and wanted to pass. Because of his soul's maturity and of all his preparation he was already very evolved in the Spirit world and able to contact his loved ones using me as his medium. He gave a beautiful and very reassuring message.

I wouldn't say that many friends come to me for readings. As I do not talk too openly about my connection and I'm not sure that many are completely aware. I know intuitively, when someone is looking for guidance on their journey and this is the area I love to help with.

I do enjoy giving messages and these messages give confirmation, but what I enjoy most is helping to enable others to find their way on their own path. Teaching others how to develop and receive and understand their own messages.

With my Spiritual friends, we often give each other messages and help each other when we can. One friend, who I met at a Psychic Fair is a great Tarot reader. She recently gave me a message. It confirmed what I already knew but I needed to hear it from someone else. As, I allowed doubt to creep in, as it often does.

I have also given her readings – generally I will connect with Red Mountain and write what he gives me for her. At first, I tried to do readings with Tarot but this just doesn't suit me. I am better suited to a direct connection to my Guides. Tarot and I just do not tango!

Message for my Mum, Lyn from Nanny Eva...
"What will be, will be Lyn, and you cannot control or alter the path that is set. The route was created in stone many years before. I love you my Lyn and give you a gift of a coin from my purse."

After giving Mum this message, she told me that only the night before she had found in her purse, a coin wrapped in film that she had taken as a keepsake from Nan's purse after she passed away.

My Mum has said of me and my connection to Spirit;
"You were always a mixed bag. You were a mixture of raver/ Spiritual quiet type, introverted and a party girl. You were never shy and always very self-assured in your own person. To me you are an extroverted introvert! You were all of the above when you felt like it, and none of the above if you didn't feel like it. You always listened to yourself and knew exactly what your soul needed.

You were always you and were never one to follow the sheep. This drove me mad sometimes, when I wanted you to conform and just fit in with life - for an easy life.

Regarding your conversations with Spirit as a child, I always knew that you were connecting, I had that knowing feeling... and I certainly believed you - as a child you were so annoyed by the constant chatter. I knew you were unable to make it up. You were so cross at times.

I feel as you have matured you have become more structured in your approach both from human and spiritual way of working.

You work well to not allow yourself to be emptied (drained) by anyone.

You are Spiritual but realistic and recognise false drama from energy vampires (lost souls) you have genuine empathy for real people, but they must be willing to help themselves, otherwise you lose patience.

I have had some undeniable 'wow' messages from you and you have connected with past relatives that have astounded me. One I remember was Aunt Liz (Nanny Eva's Aunt) you didn't even know her but described her to a 'T'. Another experience was when you gave me some Reiki whilst you lived in Corby - I actually saw two Angels assisting you and one stepping into you as you worked."

At work, I am now very careful, as to whom I share my 'secret' with. I know that so many people are either sceptical or super interested and I know it will open a big conversation. To me it is very sacred and is not something I like to talk about willy-nilly. I chose who I share this with and will only elaborate when I feel I am comfortable with someone. Too many people are far too judgmental. The thing is, I am never trying to convince anyone of anything they do not wish to believe in. Choice is sacred.

I have confided in a friend and she is fully aware of my connection and journey. She is also very respectful, she has a depth and integrity, which I see and I know that she will honour my Spirit. I will help her to develop further, as it is clear that she has a lot to discover and I am excited to guide her. She has asked me for messages and I will give them to her when and if I get them.

When chatting recently she was sharing her experiences with me and I was able to confirm things for her. I get a wave of shiver that rushes up and down my right side when Spirit is confirming what I am saying and this always helps me to know when I am on track.

It's hard though as many people only see Mediums as giving messages from dead relatives, there is so much more to Spirituality than messages from dead loved ones and I am more passionate about the teachings and philosophies that Spirit have to share with us. This was confirmed by one of my Teachers who gave me a reading.

Saying that, all these messages that I have given do give me more confidence; the surprise when something so irrelevant to me, becomes *so* relevant to the receiver.

These secondary comments are quite often the most meaningful and give the most confirmation and reassurance to the receiver.

Automatic Writing
Come Away with me – Norah Jones

Red Mountain

"You are one of us, your true self forms part of a soul, connected to a lost generation. Be that as it may, you often wonder upon it, in amazement, at the words you are channelling. For these words are of a language, when the days were darker, yet more rewarding.

We knew our purpose for the duration of sunlight; we had survival and spiritual growth to manifest, in all that we did.

There were no questions of long forgotten truths, we were following a guidance and knowing, so strong that our core was connected to the very ground we walked.

Therefore, any questions or doubts of our existence, did not create a life of lesser intention.

You the youth respected our elders. And if no sense be made from a history of torment, let it be said that a future of love will change any bitterness and resentment.

Our people lived long, and we fought hard."

'Automatic Writing' is the process, or product of writing material that does not come from the conscious thoughts of the writer.

I would add that there are two ways to do 'Automatic Writing'. The way I work is a form of dictation. I don't go into a trance generally, all I do is listen to Spirit and write the words that I am given; the words that I hear. I never allow or will anything else to control me. I do go into a Meditative state, and I quite often mentally remove my surroundings. I often write quite quickly, amazingly quickly in very swirly joined up, sometimes illegible Doctor-like handwriting during this process. I am completely unaware of what I am writing until I read it back.

Growth

"To learn is to grow,
And without growth,
You will stumble
On the obstacles of life,
Life is not an easy journey,
It is a path of constant lessons,
Keep your eyes open
And absorb all that you can."

- Red Mountain

Forgiveness

"Those that seek forgiveness,

Will never find it,

Those that live in their own forgiveness,

Will find the ability to move on,

Look within for your own forgiveness,

And not to that, which comes from others."

— Red Mountain

I have collected some more guidance and advice received from Spirit, if you are seeking this please turn to the back of the book.

Psychic Fayres
Go Your own Way – Fleetwood Mac

Eventually, I left the Housing Association; deciding to plunge myself head first into the uncertain world of self-employment. Brave or stupid I'm not sure, but I was just so fed up of feeling so restricted. I needed to try it.

As a typical Sagittarian, I am an eternal optimist. I dare to dream big and I believed that I could really make a go of it. I believed that if I worked hard enough, I could make my dreams come true.

It was risky I know but I didn't really take the time to think things through properly. If I did, I would begin to feel scared and that wasn't an option.

So, I dived in…

I travelled up and down the region, from Lincoln to Norfolk doing Psychic Fairs. I'd set up my stall with an array of colourful hippy clothes. I felt amazingly free and my creativity was flowing.

I was too scared to offer readings initially, so I set up a distraction by selling clothes. I picked them up at car boot sales and had a huge bundle sent to me from my Dad and Gloria. The only problem was, they didn't sell too well and when I finally got my Angel Cards out, it was clear that it was the readings people wanted. So, there was no excuse.

I did some very warm readings and brought comfort to many people, in amongst the tears. There is something very beautiful, about connecting with people on such a level, that your souls are talking to each other.

I remember some of the readings that I gave...

One man was a writer, and unsurprisingly Sir Arthur came forward when I was reading for this gentleman. His guidance was for this man to write more. He then told me that he wrote poetry and went on to send me some of his beautiful writing.

Another lady came to me with her daughter and I remember bringing forward a message from her husband who had recently passed over. She went away feeling calm and comforted and knowing I had helped her in her grief was an awesome feeling.

The readings took over. I stopped carting around the many bags of heavy clothes and began to concentrate on the readings. My nerves were dreadful and I panicked each time, until I got into the flow, then trust guided me.

I met some amazing people during this period and some were very supportive of my journey. Unfortunately, this didn't pay enough to cover the bills and it was time for me to do some temping again.

Red Mountain...

"This head that you have upon your shoulders has seen so much already. You have seen so much history, characters and rich tapestry.

This begins a moment of reinforced lessons for you, of which you are very accustomed to. These lessons have educated you to a level of honesty and purity, which is yet so unique and familiar.

I honour this path in which you walk, your rawness and beauty will connect with so many, as many will come to you, in order to experience and share your spirit and generosity.

There is so much that you give, that you are unaware of. Although I believe you are awakening to the strength of your character.

With blessings bestowed upon you My Child, the worst is now behind you, many lessons have been learnt, it is your time to embrace your clarity and wisdom."

Temping Again
Ain't No Sunshine – Bill Withers

ⓑ

Friends, family and colleagues have laughed at me and mocked my inability to settle in a role. I received extreme frustration from Rob and my Mum, when I would tell them I had left another job, quite often without securing another job first. I would only tell them when I was temping again, kind of like, "Oh and by the way, I don't work there anymore but it's okay, I'm working here now!"

It's like a rollercoaster ride for Rob sometimes, "Hold on tight," I'd say to him, *"Scream if you wanna go faster!"*

It's boredom that would make me bolt like a horse from an open stable door. I've literally collected so many leaving cards over the years I could start up a branch of Clintons!

This time I worked in a customer service role in a Call Centre. I was sat at a desk taking call after call from unhappy residents, reporting repairs. I sat at the same desk all day wearing a head set, which felt like it was chaining me to the desk. The building was big, grey and imposing. Just walking up to the building to start my day felt like I was walking into a prison.

This time, amazingly, I did things sensibly. I applied for jobs before I left.

I went for an interview and I waited until I had an offer. I did this for Rob as I think my rollercoaster was straining his patience and our relationship. I was trying to do things the right way this time.

Life Coaching
Everybody Hurts – R.E.M
ⓘ

I was attracted to the job advert because it was working for a company that supported people with disabilities and I wanted to be involved in something where I would be making a difference. Because Derrick had had his stroke, I knew very well what it was like to live with a disability and to care for someone with a disability. So, it was Derrick that indirectly got me started in this chapter of my life.

I started in another boring Admin role, on a part time basis. The hour's suited and family life and the school run was so much easier. However, I was still not satisfied. When would I ever be happy in a job? Why was I always unsatisfied and looking for something else? These were the questions that I was being asked by Rob and my Mum. They didn't understand the wanderlust that simmered within.

Then a role was advertised internally; as a job coach. *Coaching! This is where my Life Coaching skills could finally come into effect. At last.* I could not believe it, I was offered the role. I doubted I would be suitable, I doubted I could do it. Again lack of confidence played a big part.

I started working as an employment coach. I was coaching Job Seekers with physical disabilities. I remember the very first group that I worked with and I went on to work with a total of 9 groups before my contract and the funding finished.

I started out coaching learners on a 1 to 1 basis. Really getting to know them, taking time to understand the barriers they had. Learning more about their conditions and what skills they had; helping them to redefine themselves and to not just live by their disability. I challenged their way of thinking and offered them alternative options. We worked out what areas of work might interest them and what they needed to learn to move them closer to re-employment. I absolutely loved this work; connecting with people in a non-judgmental way.

An opportunity came along to teach the learners in groups. I jumped straight in with both feet. I would give it a go, even though I hadn't done it before. I knew I'd had enough experience, worked in recruitment, and had knowledge of disabilities; it was the obvious next step.

I would help to teach the learners how and where to look for jobs, preparing CV's, interview skills and help bring them closer to employment along with the other tutors. Once they were ready I would coach them and join them if needed when meeting possible employers; helping to bridge the gap between them and the employer.

My approach then, and still to this day, is to let people talk. I respect each and every one of my learners and clients for the journey they have been on. I feel that their voice should be spoken and heard.

Job Seekers may have had their confidence knocked and they needed to feel worthwhile again. So this is what I did, and how I worked. I wanted them to know that I was no better than them. I wasn't another stuffy professional who'd look down their nose at them. I wanted to build a mutual respect.

I taught in a style unlike what they had experienced before. I kept them engaged and interested by using language that made sense to them. I spoke and mirrored the tone of the room. Never ever patronising or condescending and always understanding and empathetic, I gave each and every one of them a time to talk and share their views, opinions and values. I chatted with them, not talked at them.

Sir Arthur gave me this message…
"You will work with many, as your voice and nature, is as soothing as a nurturing parent. A very long and well-respected career is ahead of you."

I worked with one guy, who had always done scaffolding, it was what he knew. Unfortunately, after several knee operations he was unable to do this type of work any longer. As we talked, he told me that his passion had always been in upholstery; but because scaffolding had been what he had always done, he was unsure of how to get any work or if he could get any work repairing furniture.

After learning that he had many certificates in repairing and upholstering furniture; I was keen for him to explore his skills and strengths in this area.

I think this is what quite often surprised my learners. Where the Job Centre Coaches would encourage them to take any paid work, regardless of their likes and dislikes, I would explore what made them tick, what skills they had hidden under layers of low confidence. I would listen and hear what was unspoken, regarding their abilities and disabilities. We would look into realistic options and I would help to peel back the layers of years of fixed thinking.

We looked at the beliefs that they held, and I would challenge them. I would challenge their inflexible views and ask them to question, why they thought certain behaviours were necessary and needed to be adhered to.

I gave them options and offered alternative solutions.

-

So 'Paul' came to me telling me he needed full time work and all he knew was scaffolding. I dug deep and found his upholstery skills. We challenged his idea that he needed to work full time and looked at realistic options to work with his Disability.

What we came up with was part time, voluntary work, initially. I went with him as he had an initial chat with a local employer. Prepped him along with other tutors, with a confidence building programme and we helped him to put together a portfolio to showcase his work. He was offered financial advice, so he could review his work and benefits and ensure that he did not lose out.

'Paul' went on to be offered permanent work and went from strength to strength.

-

There were many people that I worked with on this project and I gave it everything that I had. My intuition guided me to really understand the people that I was working with. It was such an honour to watch the changes in the learners as they progressed through their journey.

From the first initial meeting, and first lesson, where people would look at me with disbelief and suspicion. They were wary that I was just another figure of authority to pass judgement, and engage with a severe lack of empathy.

I had to build trust and gain good relationships with these people. The only way to work was in a 'Down to Earth', open and honest way.

As part of my development I embraced the opportunity to do a course run by The Royal Society of Public Health. It was a 'Certificate in Promoting Health'; this gave me the skills to coach people back to full health.

I also miraculously found the time to study for a Diploma in Mindfulness. I knew that if I was going to convince people of the benefits of Meditation, I would need a qualification behind me to back up my claims.

The contract came to an end and I was back in an unfulfilled admin role. Sad, feeling vey glum and as though I had gone backwards; I needed to brave the decision and use my combination of skills effectively. To do this, I decided it was time to launch Red Mountain Wellbeing.

Red Mountain Wellbeing
Sure Thing - Saint Germain Feat. John Lee Hooker
ⓘ

Following the guidance from Red Mountain, I began to teach Meditation, Spiritual Development Workshops and Reiki Treatments, through my company Red Mountain Wellbeing.

Red Mountain said....
"You are a Child of the Universe. Your soul is beautiful, and you have so much to give. We want you to teach, you have a good way with people and your ego is and always will be unaffected. Your purpose this lifetime is to pass on the knowledge that you have and help others on their journey. You My Child have come along way, we are so proud of you. From a gentle child to a woman with wisdom, we encourage you to be free from any feelings of stagnation. This is your time. You are free from the constraints of an Employer. You have shown courage and we admire you. This is only the start of your new life. There are many amazing opportunities to come your way."

Intent in the NOW...
"Do not fear for what is ahead. If you allow the thoughts to penetrate you will begin to let them sway you.

Keep your intention in the now, there is much to keep you occupied in the current moment. Why let your mind wander and take your attention from what you are living and breathing in that moment of time?

I want you to write more and to capture the very essence of what is within. Your soul has the answers and you have no need to torment yourself with lucid thoughts and worries. I want you to recapture your faith and trust. The knowing that you have when you connect to your higher self.

There are many thoughts and visions that can spoil your direction If you were to listen to them all you wouldn't step forward. My Child you have nothing to fear you are on the right path. Work will flow. Your area of strength is Meditation and Mindfulness."

I started by offering my Reiki treatments at the Centre where I worked as a Coach. Reiki has many health benefits and I felt that offering it within a healthcare environment, gave the correct message.

I was adamant that I wanted Reiki to be recognised for its Health and Wellbeing benefits. My ethos was a desire to introduce the Holistic treatments to a traditional healthcare setting and create a platform for them to work alongside each other; traditional medicine and Holistic treatment.

At the Centre there are other services that work from the Building offering care and support to service users with, Chronic Fatigue, Fibromyalgia and issues relating to Mental Health.

Reiki for me was never about promoting my spiritual side. I had never wanted to confuse the two and I didn't want to scare or intimidate people with the notion that I, or my treatment, was scary or spooky. I wore a white tunic, never any purple or velvet in sight!

As a service I promoted the health benefits, which include:

- Deep relaxation, helping the body to release stress and tension

- It accelerates the body's self-healing abilities

- Aids better sleep

- Reduces blood pressure

- Can help with acute (injuries) and chronic problems (asthma, eczema, headaches, etc.) and aides the breaking of addictions

- Helps relieve pain, and compliments pain management

- Removes energy blockages, adjusts the energy flow of the endocrine system bringing the body into balance and harmony

- Assists the body in cleaning itself from toxins

- Reduces some of the side effects of drugs and helps the body to recover from drug therapy after surgery and chemotherapy

- Supports the immune system

- Increases vitality and postpones the aging process

- Helps Spiritual growth and emotional clearing

As I continued to Meditate daily and my passion for Meditation and its benefits grew, I wanted to give others the opportunity to share this. There were no other groups in the area, so I thought about starting a group myself.

I'd been using Meditation as a spiritual tool, to help me connect to Spirit and my Guides and helpers. At circles it was always used to begin a session, and we would connect to Angels, Spirit, Unicorns and other Psychic realms. This time I wanted to create and offer something that wasn't about spirituality but purely for people to experience the health benefits and relaxation. I wanted to make it accessible to all and alienate none.

My Mission was to bring Meditation to the mainstream.

I wanted to show people that it wasn't just a hippy-dippy practice. That it held some very serious credibility for health and wellbeing benefits.

I knew from firsthand experience that Mediation could help with mental health conditions, such as depression, stress and anxiety. I had been using it to control my anxiety for many years.

For the many years I had been practicing, I was also fully aware of its relaxation benefits, as my head had often slumped during circle, as I had allowed my body to totally flop. I knew that after coming around from Meditation, I felt revived and refreshed. I also knew that it helped with physical pain too, so I had to share this secret with others, I couldn't keep it to myself any longer.

I would always start our sessions with a quick chat with each client to find out how they felt after last week's session; just as a general check in and to connect with everyone. I needed each and every one of them to feel valued and cared for; allowing people, the time to talk if they needed to. I would do the same at the end of every session; like a checking in and checking out.

The expression of people's faces when they come back from Meditation is something very special; it's priceless. A tired serene expression has replaced any tightness or tension in their faces. A look of surprise and bewilderment.

Some clients have suggested that they have really felt like they had gone away – had a holiday from their life. Some, not happy to come back – when they would have preferred to have stayed longer at the beach or wherever we had ventured during our Meditation that week.

Feedback
Zoe said…

"I have thoroughly enjoyed these classes. I leave feeling so relaxed and calm... A different person to when I walk in. I suffer with anxiety, but this has eased a lot since I have been learning Meditation at these classes. I have tried a lot of remedies and techniques to cope, but this has by far been the most beneficial. I struggle to Meditate at home but at Nicola's classes it is a lot easier, and that's with a room full of strangers! It offers an hour away from it all with no distractions. I have loved every minute and would like to attend a group every week."

M said…

"Thank you so much for bringing Mindfulness and Meditation into my life. I really enjoy going to your classes, especially on a Monday evening after a busy weekend and a Monday at work! I find the classes so, so relaxing, it's nice to be able to switch off and be taken to a special place (cliché I know!) You really are a pro at what you do x"

SB said...
"This has been one best things my husband and I have done. We have both been very stressed over the last six months, my husband on medication. Having done this class for the last four weeks, both sleeping very well, and my husband now off sleeping pills. I thoroughly recommend it and am doing so to everyone."

Red Mountain...
"Blessed are those among us that take time to sit, and just absorb the world around us. Without judgement and without comment. Just a moment of simple quiet reflection.

For those of us that immerse ourselves in the silence of a cluttered world will truly benefit from those moments of nowness.

Be still and observe before the world rushes past you, and you miss your opportunity to be part of it."

Care & Support

Cool Meditation – Third World

ⓘ

I was working with many different groups of people, some with mental health conditions, some having learning disabilities and some clients had brain injuries, some with physical disabilities and there were those that were just looking for some calm in their crazy lives.

I received some very good feedback from the groups that I worked with and provided programmes for, they proved to be very successful.

I worked with the NHS and provided a service for the Local Council doing a Home Visit for one particular lady. She was a young lady with a family and as a consequence of her physical disability, was experiencing some troubling mental health issues; because of this she was awarded a budget by the council called a direct payment. It was her choice on how she wanted to spend this money, the lady chose to try Meditation as a tool to help her. I went to her each week and we Meditated in her living room. She was not very mobile, and this was an easy option for her. For one whole hour each week I took her away from her pain and the mental torture she was experiencing. It was beautiful to see the calm wash over her face as I guided her into deep relaxation. I would leave her at the end of the session, cosy and warm in her blanket ready for a nap.

I worked with a mental health service; they would refer some of their clients to me and they would attend the Meditation sessions along with some of the staff. From what was fed back to me, the clients who came along, benefited greatly from the sessions. They experienced improved self-confidence and a renewed sense of calm.

They were all aware that Meditation was a very powerful tool, and the service I was providing was quite unique - but the majority were unaware that I was also working Spiritually.

Red Mountain guided me through this chapter and my connection to my service users was very unique as I was connecting to their spirit, which enabled me to provide a service that was indeed unlike any other.

"I took Spirituality
into the mainstream."

- Nicola Richardson

Sir Arthur Conan Doyle...

"My Daughter, how proud I am of thee. You have shone like a diamond in an otherwise dull and dreary world.

You have never given way to the obstacles that have challenged your very journey from child to woman. For it is only a true woman such as thee that can carry the weight you have had to bare.

Many will not understand the stance you have taken or the decisions you have made. Many times, there may well have been a less bumpy road to have travelled. You however, have always had a sense of immense loyalty and purpose to the true character of your soul.

For this road that you have travelled has created a woman with depth, honesty and resilience. There are many that would have fallen and given way to temptations. Not for one moment have you ever opted for the path of an easier life.

For deep down you have always known the lessons you have learnt, make you the woman that you are. You have added depth to your soul, and these layers you have built, have given protection and comfort. These layers carry wisdom, and an empathy so special, to the many lives that you cross, your nature and connection is unique.

You create bonds that enable and empower – the effect of your consciousness is refreshing and raw. Continue your work, we stand by your side.

Be bold, be beautiful, be YOU."

Meditation and Brain Injury
Trouble Man – Marvin Gaye

ⓘ

Amazingly I received a new contract which started off life in the 'Bookies'!

Derrick spoke to his friend in the 'Bookies' who happened to run a Brain Injury Charity. Derrick passed on one of my leaflets and a meeting was arranged.

This service is a fantastic organisation that helps people and their familes who have experienced head injuries. There are many different types of injury and I believe that not many people are aware of such injuries and how it can impact you and your family's lives.

I met with the service, and we discussed Meditation and Mindfulness. They had previously provided Yoga to the service users and this had gone down extremely well. So a pilot programme was agreed and I began to deliver an eight week programme of Mindfulness & Meditation.

Having discussed this with a Doctor of Clinical Psychology who was based at the Centre I was working in; he gave me a few pointers and suggestions. He was very passionate about the benefits of Mindfulness and practised it regulary with his own team. He was very supportive about my programme. I am very grateful for his support and advice.

I went on to deliver three programmes at Luton and two in Leighton Buzzard with very positive outcomes. The service users had varying needs and all were at different levels in terms of their disabilities.

To deliver this programme with any success I had to really connect with each person as an individual and tailor my delivery accordingly. It was beautiful to watch as these clients, entered Meditation and a look of peace came over their faces.

One service user in particular was extremely challenging and he tested me to the extreme. He was cynical, and untrusting, possibly traits of his character that were exagerated because of his condition. He believed there was a conspiracy and I was being paid too much to provide this service, which he also was angry about.

Each week he continued to challenge me, and question my way of teaching and the information I was giving them. I continued to work with him and the group with calmness and integrity, respecting his values and beliefs.

Out of all 12 of the group, he was one of the most grateful for the experience at the end of the programme and gave me a Thank you card. Explaining his grattitude for allowing him to experience something so special.

NHS

Teardrops – Womack & Womack

ⓓ

My next project was to be a Programme for the NHS and Luton Borough Council. I would be delivering my Meditation and Mindfulness programme into a Doctors Surgery in Luton. This was a big breakthrough and again quite a unique service. I would go in and set up my room, with my candles and Buddha, and a little scent to try to remove the smell of a Doctors surgery.

I ran several programmes and achieved some good outcomes. I had to work very hard to gain the trust of those that had been referred to me. Firstly, it was essential that I gained trust, and I did this by talking to each of them about what it was that I was doing and reassuring them that I wasn't part of the team of Doctors. I was just there to help and allow them some time to relax and take them away from the stresses of everyday life.

One client came to me with Post Traumatic Stress Disorder, and was not in a very good place. This client was very fearful and untrusting.

The NHS website explains PTSD:

"Post-traumatic stress disorder (PTSD) is an anxiety disorder caused by very stressful, frightening or distressing events.

Someone with PTSD often relives the traumatic event through nightmares and flashbacks, and may experience feelings of isolation, irritability and guilt."

(Source: https://www.nhs.uk/conditions/post-traumatic-stress-disorder-ptsd/)

The reason my client had PTSD was because they had been caught up in not one but two London terror attacks.

Immediately I worked to break down the barriers as I played Bob Marley, and we discussed the benefits of Meditation. This client had been unable to close their eyes at first, but soon into the sessions, this changed. I remember them saying, "You've changed my life."

This client had been referred many times for Mindfulness based treatment – but nothing like my programme. I was told, "You've done something different, and I won't be the same again."

This meant the world to me.

I am so honoured to have played a part in this client's recovery.

Community Work

You Do Something to Me – Paul Weller

ⓘ

I held some sessions in the community on behalf of other service providers. These were great sessions, as many of them were totally new to the concept of Meditation and Mindfulness.

I would tailor the sessions to Meditation, Mindfulness and confidence building, allowing and empowering them to find some calm and confidence before Job Interviews.

It would always start with faces staring back at me, a room full of maybe 12 people, all with a look of disbelief and suspision at the beginning of the session. By the time I had finished their expressions had changed, they had softened and I could see the change in their opinion of Meditation.

Of course there would always be the one or two that were so uptight, they were not prepared to have their view point altered at all – obviously these were the people that needed some calm the most. They would come around in their own time, I never needed to be too weighty with my guidance.

What I was teaching was something different, and most of them were open to me and the way that I taught, as it was something very different to what they had experienced before.

'Getting People Back To Work'
What's Going On – Marvin Gaye
ⓟ

As part of the freelance work I was doing I was also providing coaching for Learners with Disabilities in Northampton.

There were two clients that will always stay in my memory. The first a gentlemen, who had limited mobility due to having mulitiple strokes and a existing ongoing life threatening condition. He was, and still is, the most inspiring person I have ever met. I absolutely loved this guy and enjoyed our sessions. He had a sparkle in his eyes that said so much more than his words did. The depth to his eyes revealed a connection to a higher source; he was functioning on a different level.

He came to me for employment coaching; I suggested that he followed his spirituality; the Department for Work and Pensions and Job Centre Plus would love me - not! He was studying to be a Vicar. The reason for this direction in his life was because he'd had a near death experience.

During our coaching sessions, he would tell me all about his near-death experience.He would explain how it happened, what he felt and how it had changed his life and his direction. He and I clicked on a Spiritual level. I understood when he spoke to me about following the guidance and wisdom that he receives from God. He knew that I really understood what he was telling me and at moments we even became tearful at this level of heightened & combined understanding.

As an Employment Coach, it was my role and target to help people back into employment, but it didn't seem like I was achieving this goal here! Isn't it ironic that in his previous role, he'd been a careers advisor and now I was advising the advisor?

My advice to this client was to write his book and share his wisdom and experience.

-

I also worked with a lovely lady who I'll remember forever. She was such a sweet soul. She had come to me for help getting back into work after a knee injury.

She had always worked hard in Catering; managing kitchens and staff, but since her injury she didn't know what she could do or what she was capable of.

As usual with my inquisistive gentle questioning over the next 4 weeks, we unconvered that there were deeper issues and she actually felt totally and utterley exhausted. Her family were draining her and she didn't have anymore to give. As we spoke more it would appear to me that she was also struggling with a condition called Fibromyalgia.

So I referred her to the Fibromyalgia Support Group.

I was doing good at this whole 'getting people back to work' programme! I encouraged this lady to take some time out to focus on herself. We looked at things she enjoyed and could study to maybe improve her career options and give her more flexibility for when she was ready to work.

We talked about how she allowed her family to take advatage of her and how she was going to put in place boundries and set rules that she was happy for them to follow.

She began getting support from the Fibromyalgia support group and for the first time in a very long time, she wasn't alone. There were others who undertood how she was feeling.

This was the programme that she needed before being ready for work, so again it was tailored specifically to her. As usual, I had allowed her to steer her programme of support. I experienced many tears from this lady during our time together. Tears of relief, as she was finally being heard and had time to explain what she was really going through.

Meditation for Job Seekers with Learning Disabilities

Natural Mystic – Bob Marley

ⓘ

Again another first for me, this had been a whole period of firsts and I was learning so much from the people that I was working with.

I started to deliver Meditation and Mindfulness to a group of job seekers, who all had learning difficulties.

In the first session, we focussed on Meditation and creating a relaxing environment, with the emphasis on creating an open mind to learning new skills. The second session was more about promoting Mindfulness as a coping mechanism in preparation for the job market and working with any upcoming stressors to job searching and interview situations.

A learning disability affects the way a person learns new things in any area of life, not just at school. A learning disability affects the way a person understands information and how they communicate. Around 1.5m people in the UK have one.

This means they can have difficulty:
- understanding new or complex information
- learning new skills
- coping independently

In the group I was working with learners that had Dyslexia, Dyspraxia, ADHD, ADD, Autism and Asperger Syndrome.

As with all my programmes, I went in with an open mind and didn't really have any expectations. They were quite a young group, ranging from 16 to early 20's; therefore, I could have expected a little resistance or 'rowdiness'. What I got was respect and openness. A real willingness to engage in something new. I taught my lesson and we meditated quietly and calmly, it was enjoyed by all. They asked many questions about the Chakras and colour, and were very open to the spiritual side of the holistic approach.

On our last session we practised some Mindful Colouring, whilst listening to Bob Marley. They responded well to this session and were passionate about completing their work; certain that they would use this as a tool to help keep them calm and less reliant on screens. I know for certain that I also gained *a lot* from these sessions. Thank you to the learners for also educating me.

On the 4th March 2014 Red Mountain said to me....

"I am here My Child helping you to learn and understand your abilities. You must realise that you have now arrived, stop searching, this is where you are meant to be. This is completion, the journey you have been on, has now delivered you to this point. Your Spirituality will become teachings for others. You will be leading and taking groups. You have worked hard and now it is time to share what you have learnt. Your meditation group will be first. Well done we are proud of you, what you have achieved is beautiful. Now walk along your path and enjoy every moment."

Concussion & Whiplash
Where's Your Head At? – Basement Jax

Everything came to an abrupt end in September 2015 when we went for a short break to Dorset. It was a lovely break until I made a decision that I would live to regret. At this time, I was feeling very fraught with my business; I was unable to switch off and totally absorbed in making it work.

In reflection, I can see that I had totally swerved from my path. I wasn't Meditating any longer; teaching it yes, but not practicing myself. I wasn't connecting with Spirit to check on my route planner. Looking back, clearly I was not heading in the right direction. Therefore, something needed to change and it did… Big time.

I've already mentioned that I loved to roller skate as a teenager, and as there was a roller-skating rink at the Holiday Park, I thought it would be a good idea for us to all go skating. Big mistake to make!

It certainly wasn't as easy as I had remembered and my memories of gliding along with speed and ease were tainted hugely. Now, I couldn't skate very well at all. Even Rob was skating better than me. I was wobbling around and struggling to get any momentum and balance.

Finally, I did start to get the hang of it. Just as suddenly, I crash-landed, flipped backwards and hit my head on the concrete floor. My head had literally flipped back, and I'd given myself whiplash and concussion.

Rob came running over to me in a flash, thankfully he had given up a while ago and had his trainers back on. I was lying on the floor very dazed and confused. I'd hit my elbow and that was painful, but they had all heard the noise my head had made when it hit the floor and it was a bit worrying.

I needed some fresh air. Mum was asking me where I wanted to sit, but I was totally unable to make any decisions, I was saying, "I don't know Mum I'm really confused."

Our day ended there, and we went back to the cabin and I rested; feeling sore but okay.

We were leaving the next morning and I was due to teach a group later that next day; sensibly I cancelled. In fact, I had to cancel and postpone the whole of the next four-week program, as a few days later, the concussion set in.

I was not in a good place. I felt dizzy, nauseous, I was unable to watch TV, use my phone or a PC. It was difficult getting comfortable as my head was so tender at the back, it was difficult to rest my head on the pillow or in the bath. Along with all the uncertainty of these side effects, anxiety returned to keep me company.

As I was unable to work for the next week, I spent the time not knowing what to do with myself. I was unsteady on my feet and felt the need to walk really slowly. It was as though I had lost my confidence and I became very afraid.

As I was unable to use my phone, both talking, and messaging was a problem; I began to feel disconnected from friends and family. I experienced feelings of loneliness and was feeling quite isolated. During this time, I began to Meditate again, and this helped enormously; sitting in stillness and silence soothed my whizzing head. Walking in nature, as always, soothed me and helped me to get some normality.

I was tearful and felt vulnerable. This wasn't the me I was used to. I became half of the me I was before the fall. Because of how odd I was feeling I became even more stressed and think I exaggerated my injury holding tension in my neck and shoulders. This led on to tinnitus and loss of balance and deaf spells when I would have to sit and wait for my balance to come back. I have never felt like such a mess.

Several trips to A&E and a Cat Scan later, I was told on each occasion yes, I had Concussion and it could take years to settle down again.

To compound the stress, I wasn't working so the money wasn't coming in and the bills were piling up. Great! Fun times...

As I had done before when I was in Corby and my nerves were fried, I went to Dad's to get some calm. My Dad has a good grounding effect on me.

As soon as I landed in France I was better instantly like a magic wand. I spent the next few days sitting and meditating in Dad's forest. I wrote, read and restored my energies during the day. In the evening Dad and I drank gallons of red wine and ate good food.

The book that I read at this time was *A Mindfulness Guide for the Frazzled* by Ruby Wax. I was teaching Mindfulness and Meditation, but I needed help for myself, and this is where I found it. I left France feeling more like me, then I came home to the bills and lack of money and I slid down the slippery slope all over again. So, like always I tried to use holistic methods, and gave myself Reiki and continued to Meditate. It was all good while my day was calm but as soon as the stress levels picked up, the tinnitus and balance issues returned.

Now when I say stress levels, this also included an impending court case that my Mum and family had been anticipating. It was getting closer and anxiety was building all around me. I was trying my hardest to be a support to my Mum and I guess I was struggling under the weight of it all too.

I gave in and went to see my Doctor; I felt like such a fraud... *"Hi. My Name is Nicola I teach people how to chill out and I am in need of some extra help."*

My doctor was amazing and explained to me that I had a lot to deal with right now, had I not of been practising the Meditation and Mindfulness, I could have been in a much worse state. She praised me for my efforts and for my courage to recognise when I needed some extra support.

I went away that day with a prescription, and I am so glad I did. I wish I had of done it sooner. I didn't need to take it regularly just when I felt like I needed it. The doctor also advised me to book in for a course of massage to ease the tension in my neck, which could be causing the tinnitus. Massage helped hugely and thankfully I am now feeling back on track.

At the time, I wasn't able to work and I certainly wasn't able to help other people with my programmes and work under Red Mountain Wellbeing... I had to make a decision and it was the hardest decision to make.

So, with an extremely heavy heart, I decided to put Red Mountain Wellbeing on pause. This was not done lightly and it felt like I had lost a part of myself.

I was back on the temping train. I felt like I had landed flat on my arse and well... I guess I literally had!

Red Mountain...

"My Child you are confused and doubting your path and journey. There has been a lot of to-ing and fro-ing. I know that you are tired. You are wondering when it will all pay off. My child it is no wonder you are tired, you have given so much to Spirit and so much to the security of your family. At times, you are wondering if it is all worthwhile. May I reassure you, you are doing the right thing - keep at it. Take time to rest during this period, which we have forced upon you, it is also a time of reflection. A time to refocus your energies. Remember you cannot do everything. So now it is about choosing wisely and remember you can say NO. Whereas before you have felt the need to grasp all that was offered to you, there is no longer a necessity - it is about choosing wisely."

Life as an Office Temp

People are Strange – The Doors

ⓓ

Back into the world of temping.

There are some benefits to temping. I obviously get paid. I still feel, as though I am being true to my *free*lance ethos, and thirdly, I am free from the involvement of the office 'Dynamics and Politics'.

These 'Dynamics and Politics' are the unwritten rules, created by the staff and management, a silent hierarchy system that must be sussed out pretty damn quickly as a temp and must *always* be adhered to, if you are wanting to stay for any length of time.

These policies do not come to you via HR who may be 'aware' of this way of working but, they would never in a million years issue you with a staff handbook on this particular set of policies. These are, and always have been the unspoken rules of any office.

On arrival to your assignment all fresh faced and full of hope, you will be greeted with plenty of smiles and professionalism of the highest level. Well this is business of course. You may even be made your first and *only* cup of tea by your Line Manager. Cherish that cup, as it will be your only cup.

You will be given your log-ons, shown your desk and given some stationary. All very exciting. You will be silently sussing out all of those that you share a 'Pod' with. Everyone will have been warned to be on his or her best behaviour.

And then it begins…

You are half a day in and you begin to work out the "Dynamics and Politics" of said office.

You have been given an overview of your role by your Line Manager and shown in further detail by your Line Manager's second man. And you are left to crack on with as little fuss as possible.

On this very first day you will be included in a little polite banter, as you all size each other up. You will be asked very few limited questions on the first day; do not expect them to want to know anything substantial about you, you are simply there to complete a task, fill a chair and *blend* in.

You establish the lunchtime etiquette, "do I lunch at 12 or 1, what suits the team best?" You are responded to with a little joke "ooh you expect a lunch as well?!" We politely laugh and off I go to lunch. With the promise of returning after my lunch break!

And now, with that passing comment I am aware of the situation I am in. I can gauge that they have obviously had several temps in this position before me; some who have not returned after lunch, some who have obviously found blending with this team very tricky (hence the best behaviour warning), and some who may not have learnt the role quickly enough.

So now I know what I am dealing with. My strategy going forward is to observe, talk little and listen lots.

I return after lunch to be met with laughter and banter, "Oh you did come back then!" again we all laugh politely but I do notice the wry exchange of glances between the team members.

I finish Day One and "promise" to return for day two.

Day Two is a totally different ball game. Yes, everyone says hello and good morning. Well mostly. The extremely busy Line Manager seems happy to swerve the obligatory pleasantries. I take a seat, and off I go.

Now on the second day, the cheery banter from day one has diminished, I am no longer allowed or welcomed to join in on the friendly banter. My smiles and willingness to be included and noticed are now ignored. Here I note very quickly and sharply, my opinion, stories of relevance and humour are not wanted nor needed... It is my role, as a temp, to just laugh and smile but do not talk.

If I am lucky, I will be included in the tea run, although if there is a route out of this inclusion it will be taken. Not wanting it to appear as an obvious snub that would be too destructive to their carefully orchestrated hierarchy. Always wanting to appear as though one is friendly!

So, it appears that my 'training' has left me confused and unsure of exactly what I am doing. Now comes a huge hurdle! I have to pluck up the courage to ask for some help. I wait patiently and make myself look busy as I work out the timings as best as I can. Timing is everything. Everyone is *so* busy and unapproachable. I question whether people are as genuinely busy as they make out or is it a well-crafted aura that they portray to please their Line Manager.

I am stuck and unable to move on, I ask the question. My question is met with hostility and impatience, how dare I interrupt the flow of work?!

Before this period of temping, I had obviously been teaching and training, and so therefore I felt I had a good awareness about what people needed to be able to learn and absorb new skills. The training I was given was an overview and a book consisting of handwritten notes from the 'numerous' temps before me.

Over the next couple of days, as I became familiar with the role in Purchasing (no previous experience of Purchasing), each question or issue with log-ins and systems from me was met with sheer hostility and frustration. I was spoken to as if my capacity to remember what I had been shown *once* before, was faulty. I was asked, *"Don't you remember, I already showed you this?"* Thus, creating a little anxiety about asking for any support.

And so, I continued with the assignment quietly, making as little fuss as I possibly could.

Finally, a member of another team spoke to me and confirmed my thoughts, *"They're a tough crowd,"* I was told.

Jeez you don't say! But her words were reassuring, and it helped. Thank you to that lady who showed me a human side, when everyone else had been busy maintaining the 'Tough Crowd' image.

As I approached the last day, tension built. I could see it really was genuinely busy. Orders were coming in thick and fast. On my second from last day I was spoken to so badly. It took all I had not to explode and vent my true thoughts. It was very pedantic and totally demoralising. Now I'm sure that if it had have happened anywhere else except in that office, it would have been a true act of nastiness. However, because it happened in that office, where this secret code was in place, it was therefore deemed as acceptable and appropriate.

Well not for me it wasn't. I was another in a long line of temps that did a runner and I made *that* call to the agency.

This particular temping assignment was a worst-case scenario; you may be lucky, and you may seal a deal with a great crowd of people. People who are generally happy in their job and you can feel the vibe of the place.

Working 9-5 as a Sensitive/Empath.
Part of the Process - Morcheeba
ⓘ

After my stint temping, I began to think that I should settle down and take the easy option. HR seemed to make sense, as I was working with people and I felt there was a cross over between my training, teaching experience, learning and development. I believed this would be a good and sensible route.

I went for an interview and was offered the job 10 minutes after I had finished the interview. Just as Red Mountain said I would be. I was in the car driving away and took a call from the Director. I took the permanent role offered and it was the worst possible job ever.

What was I thinking?

One day I might work it all out. One day I might know how to coexist as a Sensitive in a spiky world. Until I work out a path that suits my sensitivity, I will struggle.

Constantly I find myself in situations that bruise my Aura, causing me to feel jaded and exhausted. As a Sensitive, I literally absorb the feelings and emotions of those that surround me. I suck up the stresses and anxieties of those that come within sniffing distance of my personal space; friends, family, work colleagues and even strangers.

As a highly intuitive person, I not only hear the words spoken, I hear the words that are unspoken. I hear the quickening breaths of anxiety, I hear the beats of a lonely heart. I see the panic and stress deep within the eyes. I feel the worry that weighs heavy in repetitive, racing thoughts. I see the grey, dense negative energy that surrounds a person's outline. My stomach will echo the tension and feelings of unease. I listen, I see, I hear; and I absorb.

I, like many highly sensitive folk, was forced to immerse myself in the 9-5. I was on the rebound from a love affair with Self-Employment which I enjoyed. Working as an Empath in the NHS was challenging and very rewarding. But waiting for the invoices to be paid and the promised work to materialise, was not so great.

So, out of survival and after my concussion, I found myself conforming and going to the office every Monday to Friday and sitting at my desk 9-5. I wore the obligatory black office trousers and any other pieces of black clothing I could find, to go with them. Struggling to find the enthusiasm to bring anymore colour into my wardrobe.

It's me, and I know it's me. This is not a cheesy break up line; *'It's not you, it's me'*. I am too flipping sensitive. Please do not think that I cry all the time because I certainly do not. Maybe if I did, it might help me release all that I absorb.

I would leave at the end of the day with my head pulsating, I'd be drained, unable to think clearly, unable to make clear decisions, with a whirlwind of thoughts, feelings and emotions being processed and repeated again and again on a loop, all the way home.

I would replay the day and the atmosphere in the office. Those feelings of highly charged adrenaline, galloping along at 100mph. Work having to be processed at lightening speeds, whether it be done correctly or not, was irrelevant. It just had to be done, actioned, off the freaking desk – pronto!

As an Empath, I felt and absorbed every part of that... *Raaaaaahhh!*

There was a part of me that wanted to run away fast. The other part of me was cross at myself for being so sensitive. *Why can't I just be normal? When will I ever conform?*

I know I am not alone in this struggle, as statistics say that at least 20% of the population also have a highly evolved nervous system and will be just like me. For those of you still finding your way through this frantic world, take solace in knowing your sensitivity is special and needs to be embraced.

Without us Sensitives there would not have been so many great achievements and breakthroughs. We are the thinkers and the creative types, who have a constant battle between our heads and our hearts. Embrace your uniqueness, we are sensitive souls.

So, it was obvious - I made *that* call to the agency again and told them I was available.

At least doing things a little more sensibly these days! I waited until I was offered a new job and made sure it was confirmed in writing. Amazingly as Spirit had told me, I was offered a job the very same week. I was offered the job at interview and it was perfect!

Red Mountain...

"It is but a time of change. A shift of energy and routine. Not a life change or move in direction. More a shift in the way that you function, routine of thoughts and internal behaviours.

Your body and your mind are tired. They are in need of a shift in gears. Your thoughts and ideas race quickly, and this has caused an effect on your system.

Notice how, and when you write, when your thoughts are in ink, the rhythm corrects itself as it should. This is no miracle. It shows how to write would impact your wellbeing.

Write everything My Child. It matters not, when you share the work, the importance is to capture what is wafting in your thoughts and creativity.

Capture, create and cultivate your work. Meditate and enjoy this heightened phase."

Message from a Great Aunt, Marjorie.

"I've come to pay you a visit my dear. You are such a sweet natured girl and will do a lot for the Spirit world. We are very excited to have you working with us. We see you becoming quite important in raising awareness of the Spirit world. You are very passionate and are building quite a network of interest. We thank you for making Spiritualism more accessible to a younger audience. I say audience, as I see you on stage delivering messages and wisdom from Spirit."

WISDOM

We begin to look for the meaning in everything. We need to walk the walk, we cannot just talk the talk anymore. It is the final battle between the Wisdom of Heart and the Wisdom of Logic.

Court Case

One Big Family - Templecloud

ⓘ▷

When my Mum finally shared her truth, it split our family right down the middle, like a deck of cards. In the Red Corner there was Mum, Derrick, me, my Uncle and his family. And in the Blue Corner we had my Mum's Father, Mother and the other Uncle and his family.

A conversation with Red Mountain after meeting with the Blue Corner...

"Have no regrets My Child, for you have nothing to question in terms of your actions. You have acted simply from the act and want of love. Think not about the actions you have taken, as you have only acted in protecting your Spirit from further hurt. Feel no remorse, as you will grow from this experience.

Allow your lessons to unfold as they deeply embed into your DNA and become a deep-rooted part of your soul. Honour your actions and be proud of your strength. From this you will advance and gather more armour.

As this is not a life of ease you will come across more challenges, but your resistance will allow you to bounce back with speed and agility.

We have watched you through these lessons and willed you to soak and absorb these lessons of the brutality that life has bestowed upon you.

"Another test,

Another journey

Another judgement

Keeping strong

Seeing afar

This is your life

You have it all

All that you need

Is all that you have."

                                                    -Red Mountain

On the first day of the court case, there was a high level of anxiety from all of us.

On this day, we did not attend court, we stayed away. I kept busy by clearing the house of clutter and taking rubbish to the tip; this cleansing process kept me busy and my mind occupied.

On day two, we went to court. As we all piled into taxis, it was clear my Mum had an army of support; surrounded by people who loved her.

This was the day that Mum was to stand in the witness box to present her story to the jury. It was her time to finally show him that he no longer had any power or control over her.

Mum and I stayed upstairs in the witness protection area. I made tea for us and gave Mum some healing beforehand. I also acted as her glamour squad; doing her hair and makeup. As Mum was called I knitted for England, keeping my mind occupied. I am still knitting it now, a scarf of many colours. I didn't even knit before this day!

It was quite poignant that as Mum left to go into court, the clock tower chimed 11 o'clock and some bongos started to play from a busker out in the street. It felt very significant and it didn't go unnoticed. They continued to play the whole time I sat there by myself knitting.

Court broke for lunch, so we went to the canteen, but not for long...

I was shocked to see the Blue Corner also sitting in the canteen, eating lunch literally at the next table to us. *How to antagonise an already tense situation?* Throw both parties together in one small room.

Obviously, we chose to leave and ate our lunch upstairs in the witness protection area.

The second day finished, it had been very traumatic for us to hear exactly what Mum had experienced at the hands of her abuser. Seeing him sitting in the box, showing no emotion or shock at what he was hearing...

I went to collect my Dad from Luton Airport, as he was flying in from France to give evidence as a witness for Mum. He arrived and I drove us to his hotel, had a quick catch up and then made arrangements for the next morning.

Wednesday morning, day three.

There was a collection of people giving evidence today. From the Red Corner; my Dad, Mum's childhood friend, two other friends and my Uncle. It was all very confusing, being in court, and knowing where to go. Especially having my Mum and Dad together in the same space for only the second time in 30 years.

Derrick and I sat in the gallery and Mum sat in the witness area with the witnesses; which turned out to be quite a blessing in disguise. My Mum and Dad had time to catch up. It was wonderful to learn that they had got on so well.

They say out of darkness, there is light.

This is certainly the case here. Much to my delight, we all went for a drink after the court case to catch up on the lost years.

Dad hadn't seen anyone for so long. So, we sat and drank many, many bottles of wine and beers. We laughed and bonded once again. It seriously was such a meaningful day for me. Medicine for all of our souls.

To have my Mum and Dad together in the same space bridged such a gap. All of my life I had sat in between their characters, not really knowing who I was. They had always been polar opposites from one another. But not anymore and now I felt connected once again to both my parents.

What bridged the gap, was the Truth.

We could all begin again.

The case continued through the week and into the next. I saw Mum's Father in the stand; devoid of any emotion as he stood in the stand to defend himself. That was very hard, and I didn't want to see anymore.

On the last day of the case I went in to wake Dylan as I do every morning. I call him King Dyl!

We were unsure if a verdict would be delivered but I told Dylan this is the last day of the court case (he knew we were at court regarding Mum's Father – but not the exact reason). Then we sat there in silence. Dylan turned to me and said, *"He is guilty Mum, the big man at the desk knows the truth."*

He amazed me. I shared this with Mum and I believe it gave her great comfort.

I have never doubted the knowledge that Dylan has. He is a wise soul and just because he is a child, I do not believe that his wisdom should be dismissed. I believe that a child can offer great advice, as they are not jaded by life yet and they view things with a simplicity that is refreshing. This uncomplicated view on life is just beautiful.

It seems there has been quite a lot of wisdom and insight to come from this case. A Detective on the case, believed a book would come from it. To explain the journey that mum had been on. It is our hope that we can help others in a similar situation to gain the confidence to speak up and speak out. Or even move closer to that point and begin a journey of recovery.

Red Mountain...
"You are free now, be the flower and light within - let your true self shine. You are over the pain - it is time to allow your Spirit to settle into a new rhythm. Allow them to live their own lessons. Again, you cannot control your own lessons, and nor can you control the lessons of others.

This experience will free you from a lifetime of confusion and bring about a clarity that will guide you into a maturity of consciousness.

Blessed be oh sweet one, lessons learnt now be free, a time of harmony will now follow thee."

The Judge wrapped up the proceedings. I had felt that he had been very gentle and sympathetic the whole way through. He gently guided the jury and they went away to make their decision.

We left.

Although Spirit had been guiding me all the way along, God-forbid the outcome had been different.

Message from Red Mountain
"We are with you completely and entirely — you and your family are surrounded in love and light. This is such a test of strength and character, not all will succeed in this test. Your Grandfather will summit into the depths of despair, as he is delivered a damming verdict.

Your Mother will rejoice as her words are validated, and confirmation of her truth is given. For all there will be justice and bridges will lead onto clearer roads ahead.

The fog will lift, nonsense will be unravelled. Love will engulf this situation. He will not walk free. God bless you children.

Replace fear with faith."

Once home, I got the call we had been waiting for from Mum…

He was found *guilty* on all 10 charges by all 12 Jurors.

I cried.

I was unable to speak.

My Mum was validated.

We had Justice.

The Harsh Winds…

"Prepare for a storm. This will be a time of judgement. The winds will be harsh, and the storms will be fierce.

There will be hurt and there will be trauma. It will not be easy - but the result will bring freedom and a strength of soul like no other.

There will be dangerous words that will create waves, but this will be a transformational part of the journey.

It is a bionic force that that needs to be laid to rest once and for all.

Great ease will come after the storm."

Publishing

Thank U Mum (4 Everything U Did) – St Germain

ⓘ

"I am here my child no need to tune in I listened to the music with you, you felt me close as I was in the moment with you.

So, you read Billy Fingers and you want to write a book and so you should I have been telling you this.

And you will piece it all together and have a masterpiece of work I know that you didn't want to use that word as it felt uncomfortable. A masterpiece is not egotistical it is a piece of work that connects in the heart of others and that is what you have."

WRITE…

Red Mountain said to me,

"Sit down and write My Child, sometimes you find it hard to connect and do not trust that it should be so easy. As I keep telling you the connection is there simple just like turning a tap on. If you wish to get messages for loved ones you will need to go deeper but for me, I am always here.

You worked well the other night - I had never doubted you. Now you must call yourself a Spirit Medium - become the title and the words that we give you. Your Coaching will change you and in turn it will change your life. You already have the basics, now you will learn to piece it all together and this will rid you of your past obstacles.

Prepare to fly My Child - as you know yourself, you have access to higher wisdom and you must embrace it. I am seeing a shift in you already, you are believing in yourself and your confidence is growing. You are becoming very powerful. Ensure that you nurture yourself. Take note. Hear!"

Red Mountain continues,

"I want you to write and enjoy the journey that it takes you on. Your Spirit is shining, and I want you to share the wisdom that you behold. Be courageous and publish these words as there are others that need these words for their own journey.

I encourage you to present these words for they are not yours alone they must be shared so that others can grow. This is your duty."

So, I ask; what am I sharing?

Red Mountain tells me I am sharing the knowledge and confirmation that Spirit exists to a point beyond vision, to a point beyond words.

"It is nothing more than feelings, emotions, a knowing and a sense of Spirit being alive in your very being. Spirit is all around you. You may not understand the words that you write but I urge you to continue.

My use of language is different to yours of today. My wisdom however, will always remain the same, and this wisdom is what I wish you to share.

You are all living in a human body. At times this body is baggage and anchors you to the realms of your Earth. When you meditate you allow this Spirit which is anchored, to travel and relinquish your earthly connection to the life that is beyond."

"The Wind, the Sun and the Rain,
Feel the Elements upon your face,
Open up, Look up to the Sky,
For while your Head is Buried,
You will miss the Opportunities that come your Way,
Open up your Heart and your Arms,
Embrace all that Touches your Soul,
Amaze in the Power of the Universe,
For You Are the Universe."

-Red Mountain

Nicola Wisdom

Spellbound – Rae & Christian

Red Mountain…

"Wisdom is not a human right,

Wisdom is something that we grow into,

We need to allow ourselves the time to ensure that,

We are, at comfort with the wisdom we grow into,

As slowly and gradually it will increase,

Around us and within us.

Shakespeare wasn't born with infinite wisdom,

Einstein didn't arrive, with a head full of knowledge,

Sir Isaac Newton was not a natural,

These souls, all found and nurtured their own journey.

For many – they will not find their journey on this lifetime,

For many they will return, to rediscover their route to internal completion,

For many it will be several lifetimes,

For many it will never deliver.

If you continue to search and receive with an open heart,

Your desire will be recognised, and your need will be satisfied,

For those, determined to arrive, have set the intention,

These are the souls, that will not rest, until their destination of certainty has been found.

For these souls – you are Blessed with adventure."

Around 5 years ago, I set up a Facebook page called Words of Wisdom, until Facebook made me change the name of the Page. On this page, I have simply shared words of wisdom. I am so proud of this page; and how it has grown. I started to share 'Words of Wisdom', phrases and pieces of writing that I knew would give people comfort.

People who have been guided to the page are from all over the world. Some of which have fed back to me, telling me that the words that I share make them feel closer to God. There is nothing but positivity and love on this page.

The more I wrote and channelled from Spirit, the more I began to share on this page. There is a lovely community Spirit and lots of joy comes from it. Not only do I give encouragement, but I also receive 'Words of Wisdom' in return. I received the post below from a friend during the difficult times I was having with the Court Case.

"You have shown wisdom to so many on your 'WOW' (Words of Wisdom) page. Imagine how that ignited something in each person to help them know, they are already strong enough, or at peace already. There is a part of you - that is already ok, already at peace and over all of this. Just tune into her and she will remind you that all is well xx Sending love today xx"

Encouragement…

"You My Child have come along way. We are so proud of you. From a gentle child to a woman with wisdom we encourage you to be free from any feelings of stagnation. This is your time, you are free from baggage. You have shown courage and we admire you. This is only the start of your new life. There are many amazing things to come and lots more work opportunities. You will write more and earn well with a regular writing feature. Your words of wisdom will give guidance and advice to others on their journey."

Waiting for the Sentence

The time is Now – Moloko

ⓘ

A difficult day. It felt as though my stomach was in knots again. I wasn't the only one; again my Mum suffered, she had been struggling with the condition Fibromyalgia and IBS. Derrick was unable to sleep. My cousins were feeling a little anxious and fully supportive of my Mum; along with all of the Red Corner.

I'd been at work today trying to figure out how to turn my 1 remaining day of Annual Leave into 4. Unfortunately, the vile man I used to call my Granddad, was still having an indirect effect on my life. I was left with such a shortage of annual leave because I had had to use my holidays to support my Mum and attend the Court Case.

I'm left with *one* day. I had intended to use it over Christmas to celebrate the joyous moments in life. But instead I was forced to use it, to attend court again.

Friday the 15th December 2017 was sentencing day.

I'm not sure this man will ever comprehend how many lives he has affected by his acts of rape against my Mum. That's right, I'm now using the word rape.

We were all anxious as we waited to find out the length of punishment the judge thought suitable for a man that raped his daughter as a child.

Not once, not twice but *continuously*. He was up on 6 counts of rape that could be pinpointed and 4 counts of indecent assault on a minor.

How could I even consider that my mind would be capable of concentrating on Friday at work, whilst the rest of the Red and Blue Corner are sitting in Luton Crown Court, waiting to hear the sentence that is given to this man.

In the Blue Corner, we had watched the denial and pretence during the trial; I cannot understand, as they continued to support such an evil man.

I had avoided eye contact with the woman that *was* my dear Grandmother. She *was* my dearest Nan. I *did* love this lady and I loved to spend time with her. It shocked me to see the coldness in her eyes during the trial.

The Blue Corner have claimed my Mum was engulfed in insanity. *I wonder if they have heard of the term Gas Lighting?* The phrase was made for the Blue Corner.

Sentencing was supposed to happen earlier that year, in November. We were told that the prison, where he was in remand, were unable to get him transport to the court. I found this very hard to believe. But no, it was a fact, the prison could not get him to the court and did not have the time to set up a video link. Amazing.

So, I gambled my last day of annual leave in the hope that the sentencing would actually go ahead on this day.

-

"Please, please, please, I put it to Spirit and my higher power, I put it in your capable hands, please let it go ahead on Friday, and let us all get on with our lives. We need closure. Let us finish the year

with closure and start 2018 with a fresh start for all of us. God Bless us all."

Closure
Superstylin' - Groove Armada
ⓘ

On Friday 15th December, we gathered and made our way to Luton Crown Court. As we arrived and passed through the security, we were searched. We made our way up the stairs to the courts.

On our way up, we met with my Mum's Barrister on the stairs. This lady is a powerhouse of legal knowledge and law. She is stern and slightly scary. Thank goodness she was on our side! She would slip into fighter mode before court began and seemingly softened a little after 'battle'.

The Barrister went on to tell us that sentencing would *not* be going ahead *again*. Mum and I stood, speechless and mouths aghast; we could not believe what we are hearing. I wanted to say to the Barrister *"Are you sure? Are you not just telling us what had happened last time, surely it can't be the same difficulties again?"*

But this is not a woman who would have any information wrong, nor is she the woman to doubt her knowledge.

We were told that due to a situation in the prison, they'd been unable to 'produce' him again at court. Mum was devastated, she needed to move on and get on with her life and this, to her, was a momentous hurdle in her ability to move towards closure.

We took a seat and decided to still go into court to see when the next date would be. I walked to find the Detective leading the case and inform him of the update from the Barrister. He was visibly shocked and told me that the courts were chaotic and full of madness that day. Prisoners had been causing big problems in the cells and the court waiting areas were full of people with standing room only. It was bedlam.

We all waited to find out what would happen next. I watched as the court Usher spoke with the Detective and instinct just told me that Sentencing was to go ahead. Regardless of what we'd been told. I watched as the Detective turned to me with a smile and gave me a thumbs up. Amazingly at the 11th hour, the prison managed to arrange a video link and we were full steam ahead.

Thankfully no-one from the Blue Corner had arrived, so we didn't have to share the waiting area with them.

We entered court 4 with the best possible situation for my Mum, a video link and no need to share eye contact with his remaining supporters.

As I entered, I saw the man that was my Granddad. My first thoughts were sadness as I saw this old, broken man sitting at a desk via a video link. He was wearing what I presume to be a prison uniform, just a beige sweatshirt. He looked thinner and I felt a little tearful, as I processed the enormity of the situation. This was no longer in our hands and hadn't been since the trial; this is in the hands of the Great British Legal System, The Crown Prosecution Service. Our country was now deciding the fate of the man that *was* my Granddad.

We stood as the Judge walked into the court. And we watched this whole episode played out in front of our very eyes. It is an episode that we can only observe, we were *not* allowed to express any emotions or make any comments.

My Mum's Barrister read out the Impact Statement. This is a statement given by Mum to the Detective, which details exactly the emotional, physical and psychological effects this trauma has had on her. My initial feelings of sadness for him, disappeared very abruptly, as he sat there shaking his head and continued his stance of defiance and denial. I am glad he had to sit and listen to this information. He needed to hear this. However much he shook his head in denial, it was an essential piece of his punishment. My Mum's voice rang loud and clear, via her Barrister and he had nowhere to hide, he was forced to listen.

I knew I hated him as he leaned forward and smiled to the camera two, maybe three times. The audacity of this man! He still believed he was above the law; still trying to manipulate and intimidate my Mum.

My feelings of hate towards him heightened as the judge continued to express his decision-making process. We heard some of the exact, graphic details that my Mum had to endure at the hands of this man.

As I sat next to my Mum, I placed my hand on her back and allowed the Reiki healing to flow. She needed comfort after hearing these atrocities again out loud.

The Judge began his sentencing and spoke of the 'campaign' of rape endured by a minor, who was in his care.

Eventually, a 14-year sentence was given, taking into consideration his age of 85.

The judge went on to explain that had he have shown remorse or any admittance of guilt, his sentence would have been somewhat shorter; however still nothing shorter than 10 years.

My Granddad reacted with nothing. Heartless and defiant until the end.

Quietly we left the courtroom with a few tears of relief. It was over. We had closure and finally at the age of 60-something, my Mum can begin her life in peace.

My Mum is a survivor of abuse and she will go on to inspire and support others. She had been heard and her journey to justice will be shared.

Open Letters
Insomnia – Faithless

ⓘ

Dear Grandfather,

I wonder, why did you think it was ok to do what you did to my Mum? Why did you believe that you had the right to rob the innocence from a child? Not just any child, your own child? What happened in your own life to make you such a bully? Did you really think it was okay to carry out such heinous acts? Did you really think you would get away with the crimes that you committed?

Grandfather, why did you not protect your daughter and allow her to grow as a woman, at the pace that nature intended? How could you sleep at night knowing that you had committed such unspeakable crimes? Did you actually sleep, are you really that heartless?

Dear Grandfather, I wonder if you feel any remorse now? Did you really think that you could convince others that you were a sweet old man? I always knew there was more to you. I always knew I didn't like you. There was something about you and I didn't like the way you operated. I kept my distance from you and observed from the side line as my Mum tried her hardest to get nurture and acceptance. I watched as nothing she did was ever good enough.

Grandfather you tortured my Mum and you need to know that it's not ok to be such a beast. You changed my Mum and muddied her physically and mentally. Thank goodness you had no effect on her spirit and soul for they remain as pure and strong as ever.

~

Dear Grandmother,

I loved you. I don't anymore. We would chat and share a bottle of red. Never again. I miss my Nan.

You have turned your back and chosen a side. You chose your destiny Nan. Why did you not see what was plain to see? Why did you not see the pain in your daughter's eyes? Grandmother, what really goes on behind your tormented smile? For years I have wondered what goes on behind your vacant eyes. Did you not see the sadness hid by your daughter? How can a Mother not see the despair in their own child's words – when she confides in you her secret, at such a young age? Not just her father but her Grandfather too.

Dear Grandmother, why did you ignore your daughter's confession? How do you feel now? Are you sad that you have lost us, or do you not care? Can you see the truth now through his web of lies?

EMPOWERMENT

It is the time when we have a choice.
We can either listen to our ego – stop evolving and begin to decay or we follow the voice of our higher self and begin to cooperate with Nature through realizing our own creative potential that was given to us at birth.

The Future...
Due Tramonti - Ludovico Einaudi

Red Mountain…

"Please do not question any longer – your journey or your purpose. For my child if you continue to question and delay, you will lose momentum and certainty.

A book is already within you – all that you need to do, is piece it together and resolve to complete it. A gap of any length will discourage you and you will struggle to return.

Call upon me, as you have been doing – you have returned to your prayer and your voice and thoughts have been heard.

For you there is no option, other than to write, work will come along and fund your written work until completion. A publisher will surprise you, as your written work, is gifted with readers.

Your work will travel far, and your audience will welcome your work. There are many more waiting to receive your shared words of wisdom."

"The breath that you take,
is the pause that surrounds you."

-Red Mountain

EMPOWERMENT

"In our silence we cast our judgement, in our judgement we send out our thoughts, ensure that your wisdom is restricted by none."

"Thoughts and prayers are with you my child. Your journey has been erratic, and you have endured much stress. Your troubles have given you lessons in life, and content for your writing.

Allow us to settle once again to a rhythm that allows your connection and substance to value that your soul desires.

You have deviated from the path, that was intended and, lost you have felt. This new direction that you are heading will allow us to reconnect and add value to your rightful intention.

You my dear have drifted and we needed to bring you back to source. Your objectives were blurred, and your Aura was cloudy.

Your vessel is full and empty you must, we see and feel your tiredness as only we would.

Making time for you is as essential as breathing."

"Ask and it will be given,
Believe and it shall happen,
Trust and you will not falter
Allow and you will be guided.
All that you need will be given,
Be thankful and allow the consequence,
To provide you with the power,
As the magic creates a system to carry you through,
Many years of worry and anxiety,
Have created a tension and uncertainty,
No one will ever understand all that you have put yourself through.
And why we allow ourselves to function in this state is beyond me.
Let it all go, it is out of your hands – and always has been."

-Red Mountain

Gone, are the days of being stuck all day in the dreaded office.

Thankfully I am now delivering Meditation sessions again and have a great group of people I am working with. It is my calling and I feel as though I am back on the path I am supposed to be on.

When things click into place as they now are, I cannot deny I am being gently guided, and opportunities present themselves to me, I am receiving them with open arms and gratitude.

Sometimes I smile to myself as I watch and observe life, I am secure in the knowledge that Spirit have great plans for me and I give thanks.

Guidance

Control…

Control - Why must you feel as though you need to control everything? This sense of needing to control creates a tension within your Solar Plexus, which has a knock-on effect and powers digestion problems. Each moment that you breathe away the need to control you feel your stomach release and a softness that follows.

You have no control over the Universe and you allow it to unfold with trust. Trust and have faith in the flow. You are burning energies unnecessarily and this is impacting on your wellbeing. You must sow the seed then let it go.

Patience is required allow things to pan out as it should - remember my words you will be surprised at how things flow with ease.

Good fortune is coming to you My Child as your leg work begins to pay off. Your writing will flourish, and money will be plentiful you and your family will travel, and creativity will pour from you.

Allow thing to take shape and let go of control.

People Pleasing…

Pleasing other people - not an easy feat. Why must you base your happiness upon the happiness of others. Firstly, you must ask yourself - by bestowing this sentiment to another will I gain happiness within. As before you go on to please others, you must ensure that there is happiness at your own core. As all that you give could taste bitter.

You are looking for your own happiness by pleasing another, which will never come. Nurture your inner happiness as a paramount. And genuine happiness will trickle and filter through without condition.

"Speak Clearly,
Know your truth,
Look around you,
And share your love."

A Winter's day all blowy and stormy

So much for the forces to blow away. Energies to be refreshed and emotions to be removed. A time to be still as the storms circle overhead. All necessary to strip bare all that has gathered.

Removal of worries and burdens.

Stand out in the wind and rain and allow yourself to be charged by the process of clearing and cleansing - right back to bare branches.

These winds will pass over and a new energy will bring a focus for the changes ahead.

A time of reinvention and clarity - a focus so clear, the mind will be sharp and free from memories that have held you back.
Embrace the extremes and allow nature to soothe and de-clutter.

For next brings in understanding and empathy - a state of stillness. As the phase begins you are surrounded in love. Take time to be still and nurture your energies - the light and the freedom is within your grasp.

"Have no doubts - positive you must be,
The worst is behind you,

A new beginning you will see,
You have endured the very hardest,
No more will you allow,
The Woman in you,
Steps forward - with her head held high.
Surrounded and protected
Go forward with courage and Love from above."

The Complexities of a Raw World…

It hasn't always been the same way of living, as it is now. Today there is much to strive for and much to aspire to be.

Many years ago, we lived a life of simplicity and survival. We were not looking – to be better than the person we were yesterday, nor were we looking to be better than our neighbour or our colleague.

Today the complexities of a new and ever-changing world cause havoc and chaos.

You must learn to loosen your grip on the reigns of life, have faith that the flow will take route just as it should.

No amount of forced control and desire will change or alter the flow that is intended.

Admire your neighbour – but do not judge or measure your goals against them.

Let life flow, and it will work out just as it should. By releasing your grip you lessen your urgency to live your life, and begin to – just be, being mindful and steady, living beneficially to your soul.

There is no such thing as perfection and no amount of forced control will ever provide a 'perfect life'.

Take time to enjoy the imperfections of your crazy little life. It is your Life. Live it.

Suit your Soul…

Many meets along the way. Many Characters will mingle and migrate. Many souls will embrace and entangle.

Many wishes, hopes and fears will dance in the atmosphere. Many notes will bounce and circle creating waves and vibrations.

Which of us will ever know for sure - which of us will ever be entirely certain. With so many paths to follow and so many instructions to work through.

It is only a wanderlust that will keep you searching for the life that you are hoping for.

You must continue to dance and turn with all your glory, until you find the way to suit your soul. With a persistence that will keep you from settling for anything less.

Others will judge - they always will, but that is no reason to bow down to confirmation.

Conformity is not the life for you, your life must contain adventure and beauty. Nature and Nurture.

Simplicity is key - but bland is will not suit. A gentle life of creation and beauty will nourish your soul.

Riding on the waves of love as you recover from past hurts and rebuild your strength again.

To ask what is right for you - put the question to the universe, you will know in your heart what is right for you.

Skipping and dancing, keeping your heart light will bring you closer. Fun and laughter will help you to recover and restore energy levels to regain balance.

A New Year of choice for you creates a Future with Freedom.

What Will Be – Will Be…

Living this life, momentarily,

I wonder, and allow my thoughts,

To run free, gathering gently.

What am I expecting?

What will be - will be.

I shouldn't force an anticipated outcome,

What am I expecting?

What will be - will be.

I have no control over, what is meant for me,

So gradually, I learn - and no longer expect,

For now, I have found, my faith, and my trust,

As this journey pans, out, I sit back and observe,

What will be, will simply be.

All the time in the World

Have no regrets My Child, for you have nothing to question in terms of your actions.

You have acted simply, from the act and want of love.

Think not about the actions you have taken, as you have only acted in protecting your Spirit from further hurt.

Feel no remorse as you will grow from this experience.

Allow your lessons to unfold as they deeply embed into your DNA and become a deep-rooted part of your makeup.

Question not your intentions as you have acted only with the protection of your Spirit at the forefront.

Honour your actions and be proud of your strength. From this you will advance and gather more armour.

As this is not a life of ease, you will come across more challenges, but your resistance will allow you to bounce back with speed and tenacity.

We have watched you through these lessons and willed you to soak and absorb these lessons of brutality, that life has bestowed upon you.

You have the power to rise above all, and even more if you have to. Know for certain you have an inner strength that is strong - yet still sweet, damaged - but not bitter, and bruised - yet not spoiled.

Your strength is illuminated as you pass through this phase. We honour your Spirit, and hold out our hands, you have reached the green pastures, with new chapters ahead.

It is for you to re-write the next phase, as the old habits no longer have a place within you. Going forward you have a clarity and wonderment surrounding you.

Another test, another journey, another judgement.

Keeping strong, seeing afar, this is my life.

I have it all, all that I need, is all that I have. You are not just the creation of another, you have your own path to follow. Now is your time to untangle and free yourself from the layers and webbing of history.

You must make your own blueprint, where there are no conditions. The limits are endless.

Do not confine yourself to the limitations set by others. It is a time to honour your own boundaries. What is it that you want? What is it that you must do? I ask you to ponder on these questions. No need for immediate answers - you have ALL the time in the world...

Letting Go in Trust…
You are indeed working for Spirit, and with your sensitivity you are able to connect on a deeper level with more understanding and a growing oneness.

This does not make you more superior than others, and nor do you wish to be more superior. This is merely to do with your journey and your own development.

As you understand yourself more and the way that your Spirit needs to be nurtured. You will know and recognise the ways in which your Spirit craves gentleness.

You are not a delicate soul with no backbone, in fact the complete opposite. You have fighting Spirit and are fearlessly protective over your Spirit and it's needs.

This sensitivity is a gift - and now your awareness will grow, as will your assertiveness.

My Child now begins a new chapter for you. I sit back and watch with love and pride. As this knowledge leads you even closer to the source.

As you take the steps that have been laid out for you. You are walking your own path of Spirituality as your fellow brothers have previously walked before you.

You will go on to philosophise and spread an inner wisdom. We urge you to continue. The subtle changes within are helping you to understand yourself even more. Before you have blocked but now you are encouraging.

We ask you to grow with self-belief and faith. You owe it to yourself to let go and trust.

Expectations...
Begin to write let the words flourish into the air.

As you begin to flow, the words form as thoughts, darting and dancing, free in the stream of a dream.

You go about your day and often wonder how you manage.

With the trials and tribulations and the dramas of life.

With elegance, courage and pride the only way you know. For life is never easy and your heart will feel the sorrow of expectations placed upon you.

Forget the expectations of others for they matter not.

What really is important is the expectations you place upon yourself. Make yourself happy in this lifetime, live the life you know you should, and allow your inspiration to guide.

This is a life of two sides; both beauty and despair.

Have no expectations of perfection and you shall not endure delusion.

Live a life of simplicity, for heavens knows, dealing with egos daily can be complicated and confusing.

Blessings be bestowed upon you.

From Sir Arthur Conan Doyle

A Time of Reflection…

"*My dear I am here waiting for you, we sent you a gift of flowers, for we were waiting to work with you. You have been busy leading your life and we understand this.*

But my Dear, you also have a job to do for us in Spirit. You have opened your soul to the connections and chords that bond us.

My Dear we send our love and healing thoughts to the people affected by the Himalayan disaster. It is a time of great sorrow. Even though our bodies are no longer earth bound, our concerns grow ever more.

We ask that as a collective your group of healers send your prayers, as the power of your combined energies, will reach far. To the survivors, families and those that have passed over, may their transition be smooth and comforting.

It is a sad time and a time of reflection and shared concern.

We can offer no answers as to why this has happened, we know not, what the Master Power make of this disaster. This devastation will bring many questions and raise many doubts.

We must seek quiet reflection to heal with thought and intention.

God bless these souls."

Awoken to Spirit…

You are a child of the Universe, you have the Earth residing within you.

At times you may need to step back and asses your learnings, and re-ground yourself.

EMPOWERMENT

You will all get lost in the chaos and commotion of a busy life, but it takes real strength to step back and take time to be still, whilst, all around you remains continuously charged.

It is with this knowledge that you are able to recognise that, which your soul is craving, and provide the nurturing that is so desperately needed.

Do not fear, this is not a time for your path to abruptly end, your journey will continue. Remember all wanderers, explorers and travellers will need to take rest.

Your world is chaotic, and it is not a path of smoothness. There will be many bumps and dilemmas along the way.

Your people are often in a hurry to complete their journey, however, this journey will never come to an end, for while there is forever Spirit, there will always be knowledge to be shared.

I praise your people who give their dedication to Spirit, but I urge you to keep one foot grounded as whilst you walk the Earth Plane, grounding is a matter of survival.

There are many who look on and have little or no understanding of the way that we work with you. To some, an element of mystery remains, but to those of you who have woken, your world will be a purer place.

I know many will not tolerate the small-minded ness of others, but with your open heart and kindness, you must send love to these people. Even if the words they speak wound and offend, it is their own lack of understanding. We must send them love, as they have not evolved as you have beloved ones.

Make not, sounds of jealousy,
Make not, sounds of bitterness,
For these emotions, will only hinder your growth,
Continue with forgiveness and hope,

NATURAL MYSTIC

Draw upon the Earth for guidance,
Listen within, to steer your soul,
You will always know in your heart what is right.

Blessed be Sacred Ones.

I have nothing more to say - God Bless my Children.

Come Rain, Come Shine,
Walk on, Be Free,
Have Hope, Love Hard,
Live Strong.

Being a Sensitive…

"Begin to think and allow your creativity to flourish to the surface. This creativity is what will allow you to become the person you have always wanted to be.

As I say these words to you feel the emotion flow as we Spirit touch upon your Spirit and recognise your true calling.
This calling is no longer a desire to be the creative you... It is a calling of home coming, recognition and whole ness.

These words that form, these words that become your inner wisdom and inner guidance are to be shared.

Your life has not been an easy or simple journey. You have been sailing on the emotions of others.

You are sensitive and show your compassion and heart felt understanding of life and all that it throws at people.
Your eyes are open, wide open, and you not only see the torment in others, you feel it.

I suggest to you My Child a period of calm, a time to step away from the emotions of others.

Not that you do not care, rather that you care too much.

Along with the help of Spirit, you must take time to care for yourself. Your inner beauty needs some time to restore. It is time to rethink the work that you do..."

"Be you, be at one,
Be honest, be brave,
Be open, be free,
Let Spirit Guide you
Be with thee."

Un-comfort Zone...

"As you go about your daily routine, ask yourself - What can I do differently today?

Why must most days mirror that, of the day before? Each day we must challenge ourselves to go about our "routine" in a different way.

This situation which we refer to as "comfort zone" may be preventing you from living the life or being the being that you could be.

Be bold be brave, for you can make a difference, dare yourself to think and look at situations from a new perspective, Look for the miracle in each day"

Namaste.

Balance of Life...

Begin to write I am told "my dear."

So, it's not always easy, being a mum, a wife, working and juggling life. Along with the constant pull towards my Spirituality.

You see, it's got to the stage in my journey, where my Spirituality seems to be the biggest draw and demand on my day... As, along with the love for my family, it is where my heart is.

I seem to struggle with the day to day... It doesn't have the same meaning to me anymore. Life is deeper, and I look at things from a different angle.

Those things, that may seem important and super urgent to others, just don't have the same effect on me.

My head, heart and my Spirit are now functioning on a different level.

There is a contact battle with my "earthly" commitments and yes, the need to work my "day job" to help to support my family and the need to connect and honour my commitment to Spirit.

I have been developing for many, many years - I was also blessed with a connection from childhood, but along with my development, and understanding of life, I now have a strong desire and sense of duty to share this knowledge.

I am aware that not all, are ready to progress and some even enjoy their state of rigid ness. They may think I am losing or lost it! ... This is where my confidence comes in - I have no need or desire to seek approval from others.

It is my journey and I am passionate about my journey. No one will persuade me otherwise.

With my certainty and connection to Spirit, I feel such a sense of serenity. I go about my day as though I am not totally grounded, probably I am not, that's the reality...

I avoid the media and the news. Yes, I have an awareness of the events worldwide. But it is my choice and I prefer not to let them come into or effect my energy.

Ok so some might say I am living on "cloud cuckoo land". Again, I care not.

From day one I have always thought about things, in a non-conventional way, and I guess I continue to do so. Never being able to conform and unable to follow blindly.

Some rules imposed on me making me want to run   A need for bare feet and freedom. There are those that won't get this - but I know there are others that will wholeheartedly understand.

I am a sensitive and therefore, my senses serve me well. I will continue to work this way and soak up the learnings and knowledge that Spirit pass down to me.

Until I create and implement that perfect balance between my 'day job'and my souls desire I shall be torn.

So 'my beautiful guides' I leave it with you to guide and orchestrate - and I will watch this space...

God bless you,

Namaste.

Changes...

Another new day... the shadows of yesterday are a memory. What did I learn yesterday that will carry me forward into today?

I learnt yesterday that I am embarking on a period of change. With the help and guidance of Spirit - things are about to change.

"You are leaving behind you, times of uncertainty. A new dawn is emerging. You are like a butterfly, and have been emerging from your cocoon, now you begin to spread your wings and allow yourself to fly.

All those doubts and uncertainties are shedding and leaving your true beauty and wisdom exposed. Your vulnerability has left, and a strong beautiful woman is emerging.

Let yourself fly freely as we will carry you on the currents of Spiritual certainty.

We are blessed that you have chosen to walk this path and we will take care of you as you continue this journey.

You have given so much and learnt so much, and now you will begin to see the fruits of your dedication flower and blossom.

Be proud my child as you have learnt so much. Always there is more to learn, but life is on a new aspect for you now. You will not go back to old ways of thinking and being. You have the strength and tenacity to allow your knowledge to guide you.

A new chapter of enlightenment will follow when body and mind are connected... This is what awaits you.

Be patient and enjoy the process as you have enjoyed the previous chapters.

...Your journey continues. God bless you my child."

Mindfulness – be present in the day
So, what is this feeling I have about me today?
A feeling of heaviness, a lack of motivation and a feeling of stillness. It seems that my mojo has given me some space today.

I ask Red Mountain to connect and give me some clarity on these emotions and the sense of numbness about me today.

"My child you cannot expect to be bouncing with joy and motivation each and every day. Life is about balance and you will need days like this to process your thoughts and experience all aspects of your personality.

Yes, generally you are a motivated person, but today your soul craves some rest and rejuvenation.

You work with many different personalities and it is bound to take its toll on you. You cannot give your all and not expect to come crashing down at some point. It is not a case of licking your wounds, as there is no self-pity involved - just a time for reflection and reassessment.

As I have said to you before you must feel these emotions and not block or self-medicate to achieve the ability to "zone out" - you must feel and breath through these emotions.

At times you are too harsh on yourself and you set yourself targets and goals that cause you to become too focused forgetting the simple pleasures in life.

For one day forget about the big plans and ideas - let your mind rest and acknowledge each part of this day as though you are a true part of every minute of the day. This is living in the moment and this is what your body craves for the day.

There you go - your guidance for the day. Breathe and be present.

Tomorrow is another day and the plans and ideas can create once again.

A Personal Message from Sir Arthur Conan Doyle

The urge to write this morning has been over whelming. I guess this is my message from Spirit, to start writing.

The encouragement is from Sir Arthur Conan Doyle, it is he, who told me to introduce himself into my writing. So, this morning I am sharing a piece from my journal, as per my instructions.

A conversation with my Guides from October 2014.

Red Mountain tells me he is with me (My Child), he tells me there is no need to connect further. "I want you to know that your connection is quicker and no need to drag it out."

Sir Arthur tells me "Yes My Dear I am with you, and time for some answers."

How do I protect myself when working?
Sir Arthur Conan Doyle tells me that I will need to block my Solar Plexus and ground myself each morning, I must look to Spirit and ask for protection. I am told I will learn, and that I am getting closer. I must ask Spirit to help me work on an Earthly Level (during my day job) and not allow myself to work on a Spiritual Level.

I am told that the teaching I do in my (day job) is all part of my journey. And as I work more on an Earthly level it will become easier and not so draining.

My Spiritual Teacher has recently sent me an image, Sir Arthur tells me this image is a symbol of my strength and courage to go it alone. He tells me I do not need the reassurance from others, when my higher self is guiding me. He knows that I listen and tells me this is my independence. This is my freedom on my continued journey.

"Remember My Dear I am here for your development and guidance and not for the drama that comes with others. These are for you - your lessons to figure out.

I am told that I have this gift for a reason and this must be encouraged and nurtured.

God bless you My Dear."

A Conversation with Spirit...
As I sit here in the presence of Spirit, I allow my energies to attune, to blend and let the communication commence.

I sit in a candle lit room with my Spirit Guide Red Mountain. We sit on the floor upon a beautiful thick sheepskin rug with our legs crossed.

I have the option to speak with Red Mountain and further my knowledge with his infinite wisdom.

We sit quietly at ease in each other's company.

I ask him to share with me more about his time on the earth plane.

He tells me, *"It was a time of great love and Great War. It was a passion that run deep through the culture of my people. The passion was a need to defend and protect the land from the authorities. We would fight to the death to protect our sacred land. And we often did.*

Our land was our energy centre - we woke with the sun and worked our land to benefit our people. We celebrated our land and the harvests - you could say that we were similar to that of the pagan people of today who work in line with the seasons and nature.

Our people told stories of generations gone by. We shared our time on your earth as best as we could. It was our duty to prepare the next generation with a knowledge from times gone by.

Amongst our people was a kinship like no other. We had a connection -deeper than that of you, and your neighbour - we shared a deeper understanding of our reasons for walking this earth and what our duties were, and what lessons we were sharing.

We would seek and find the brother who would help us with the knowledge that we lacked, and we would in turn share the message that was meant for him.

Life was Spiritual and simple - today you have so much, but the fulfilment in life seems so much less. Unless you are walking the path that the great Spirit intended emotions can be unbalanced.

To gain the balance you must go back to the seasons, be mindful of the movements of your earth. Look deeper into the storms, for each storm has a message and a lesson to be understood.

I want you to understand why you are here - what is the great plan for you. I know the answer - but it is for you to understand?

Once you have your understanding everything will work together as your priorities will shift and your life will become more purposeful.

Go forward amongst the trees and the dark. As you brave the unknown your courage will grow.

Your strength will gather momentum, and your heart will experience more love, with this momentum and experience your limits are endless."

On the waves of Life…

Be a surfer on the waves of life, who knows where it will take you, who knows where it will lead you.

There is only one thing you can be certain of, and that My Child, is that it is your destiny and souls' purpose to lead you on the path, that which is meant for you.

Have faith in your direction, when you are connected to Spirit, we will not see you lost at sea.

For always you can turn to us and seek direction and guidance. We are steering you on your path with our hands upon your shoulders. All that you need to do is listen.

Listen within to the voice that gently whispers with certainty and calm. For this is the voice of Guidance from the Great Spirit.

It is to be heard but only when a man is ready. For not all have the ability to recognise this guidance, as the life force that is carving your journey.

This lifetime is a voyage of wisdom and experience - a gathering of knowledge. As your soul ages and your wisdom deepens your lifetimes lessen.

A Personal Journey…

As I write this guidance from Spirit, I question whether it the right thing to do - to share these very personal words of guidance and encouragement.

But the urge to write these words and organise them in some form of logical order for my own reference is leading me to continue. I have piles of paper all around me with scribbled pencil, it is time to give these words the honour they deserve.

These words of encouragement are from Spirit and the encouragement is by no means from a place of ego.

I am told by Spirit that my Wisdom is growing (My Child as referred to by my Spirit Connection). These Words are to be circulated widely and according to Spirit will be published in print. Spirit tells me the Words that I share will help people - people in therapy, people on their journey and people with addiction. My Guide tells me this shared wisdom will become their Wise Counsel.

Spirit tells me I am on the right Path, and that my knowledge and skills will supersede those around me. I am to speak from the heart and use my own inner wisdom as it is unlike any others. These words from myself and Spirit will become desired.

EMPOWERMENT

"My Child - you are on a rocket of life powering you through the universe.

Those that think they can't - can't,
Those that think they can - can,
Take a moment - step back,
And decide are you a Can or a Can't?
The Cant's miss opportunities,
And the Can's create opportunities."

Inspirational Words of Wisdom

To be at one is all that we ask,
Take control of your creation,
You are a leader - walk with your head held high,
Do not look behind you - keep walking forward,
Take another man's hand, empty of negativity and be free from pain,
Show me your trust and I will show you - your future of happiness and wisdom.
Do not doubt have courage,
Draw from the deep resources within,
Let not, the Master Be your guide - guide yourself from within,
Have fun and enjoy the journey,
Let it take its course,
Keep humble and you will do no wrong.
With love and peace.

Winter Solstice...

"As you begin to write and feel the pen move across the paper, you can begin to recognise and release any uncertainties that may have been holding you back. For now, you are no longer a prisoner to your insecurities, for now you are no longer a stranger to the world beyond that, which you once knew ...

Feel the freedom and the new energy as it takes hold of your dreams and turns them into reality - the reality that you once dreamt of.

It is your reality and you are a Master, of this Life that you create for yourself, for you and only you - know the journey in your heart that you must take.

There is a reason for this journey. As you know every step takes you closer to the Spiritual Divine.

You walk a path that is lined with Opportunities and Obstacles, only you know what it is, that your souls journey needs to experience, for only you alone can walk this path.

I urge you to continue - as you do, the doubts become less significant and your courage grows stronger.

It can be a lonely path in terms of your solitude in thought and Wisdom. But know that you are never alone - you will feel the gentle hand on your shoulder as Spirit walk with you.

You are a Warrior of our people - continuing the messages of Love and Eternity.

For the Power of the Essence is Simply Devine."

A Footprint of Truth and Compassion – Red Mountain

My child, you are all that you need,
You have the power residing within you,
Do no look to others - for you will be disappointed.
You are enough. Everything that you need is,
Everything that you have.
Physically and mentally you have unwavering strength,
No longer do you need or seek the approval and acceptance
from parents or elders,
The focus now, is about living and breathing your own truth.
The path that you walk is a creation from within your soul,
There is not another direction that would bring you to
Such completeness,
This path is a direct route to your path home.
Never have you understood so entirely where your comfort
lies,
This for you is an act of certainty and a knowing,
For as you follow your heart, in bewilderment,
The opportunities unfold before your very eyes.
Speak your simple truth My Child, and continue to act with
kindness,
To others and yourself, your energies will be enriching,
As you leave your footprint,
Your intention is one of truth and compassion.
An understanding of human behaviour, is nothing but - unique.
Continue - just, as you are.

Glossary

Angels and Arch Angels

"An Angel is generally a supernatural being found in various religions and mythologies. In Abrahamic religions and Zoroastrianism, angels are often depicted as benevolent celestial beings who act as intermediaries between God or Heaven and Earth. [1][2] Other roles of angels include protecting and guiding human beings and carrying out God's tasks."

"An archangel is an angel of high rank. The word "archangel" itself is usually associated with the Abrahamic religions, but beings that are very similar to archangels are found in a number of religious traditions. The English word archangel is derived from the Greek ἀρχάγγελος. It appears only once in the New Testament in the phrase 'the archangel Michael'."

As the cards had been advising me I am a healer and a counsellor and that I needed to study. My next obvious adventure was a course in counselling. I went every Thursday night to college, and I loved this course. It made so much sense to me, and I knew from this that I wanted to help people. I honed my listening skills and began to think about things differently. My mind was again, opening even further.

Archangel Ithuriel:

Meaning: I am alight. Colour: All the colours of the rainbow but especially, blue, violet and pink. Angel of self-love and self-development he leads you gently towards letting go of everything you no longer need in your life which is holding you back from reaching your full soul potential.

Archangel Zadkiel:

The angel of mercy. He encourages and motivates people to turn to God for the mercy and forgiveness they need to heal from pain and overcome sin, freeing them to move forward with their lives in healthier ways. Zadkiel also helps people remember what's most important so they can focus on what matters the most in their lives.

Archangel Raphael:

The Angel of Healing. He is symbolised by the colour green. A deep and intense Emerald green shade.

Archangel Michael:

The Angel of Protection. He is symbolised by the colour blue.

Clairaudience

The supposed faculty of perceiving, as if by hearing, what is inaudible.

Colours of The Chakras

    Red - Root Chakra

The first of the seven energy centers, Muladhara is also the most dense of them all. The main colour of this chakra is red which is also the most dense colour of all. Learn about the meaning of red and discover the less known second colour found at the centre of muladhara.

    Orange – Sacral Chakra

Orange is the colour of your second chakra, which is located bellow the navel. The main energy of this colour is creativity and feelings. Explore the colour of your sacral chakra in depth and discover the gifts and challenges of orange colour.

Yellow - Solar Plexus Chakra

The centre of our being - the colour of sunshine and the colour of the third energy centre - the solar plexus chakra. The main energy of yellow is intellect. Do you like yellow colour? Discover what yellow means and how it manifests in your subtle body, at the solar plexus chakra.

Green - Heart Chakra

It is the colour of healing, balance, tranquillity, and serenity. Green brings wholeness to our lives and it is the colour most frequently found in nature. Explore the heart chakra colour and discover its meaning.

Blue - Throat Chakra

The throat chakra is the fifth chakra. It is one the three primary colours. The main energy of blue is communication and it is the colour used to soothe the soul. Explore this Divine colour in depth, learn what blue colour of the throat chakra means and how it manifests on all levels of your being.

Indigo - Third Eye Chakra

The sixth energy centre - your third eye chakra. It is the colour that opens the consciousness and brings awareness to higher planes and connects us with the Spiritual world. Discover the hidden meanings of the third eye chakra indigo colour.

Violet - Crown Chakra

Violet is the colour of cosmic awareness and cosmic consciousness. It is a unifying colour, the colour of oneness and Spirituality. The energy of this colour is very healing and can soothe away pain.

Learn more about this Spiritual colour and its manifestation at the crown chakra.

(Source: https://www.chakra-anatomy.com/chakra-colours.html)

Dukkha (Pāli; Sanskrit: duḥkha; Tibetan)

An important Buddhist concept, commonly translated as "suffering", "pain" or "un-satisfactoriness". It refers to the fundamental un-satisfactoriness and painfulness of mundane life. It is the first of the Four Noble Truths. The term is also found in scriptures of Hinduism, such as the Upanishads, in discussions of moksha (Spiritual liberation).

(Source: Wikipedia)

Gaslighting

Gaslighting is a form of manipulation that seeks to sow seeds of doubt in a targeted individual or in members of a targeted group, hoping to make them question their own memory, perception, and sanity. Using persistent denial, misdirection, contradiction, and lying, it attempts to destabilise the target and delegitimise the target's belief. *(Source: Wikipedia)*

Meditation

    Eagle Symbolism:

As a power animal, the Eagle is most frequently associated with wisdom and freedom. Here are additional symbolic meanings for the Eagle totem:

Intuition, Creativity, Strength, Courage, Hope, Resilience, Healing, Vision and Healing.

GLOSSARY

(Source: http://www.Spiritanimal.info/eagle-Spirit-animal/)

The Anchor symbolises:

An anchor is a heavy weight that holds a ship in place. Remaining firm and steadfast amid the uncertainty of storms and the elements, an anchor symbolizes such concepts as firmness, tranquillity and hope.

In a Spiritual context, the anchor symbolizes "the stable part of our being, the quality which enables us to keep a clear mind amid the confusion of sensation and emotion. an anchor symbolizes such concepts as firmness, tranquillity and hope.

(Source: http://www.religionfacts.com/anchor)

PTSD

"Post-traumatic stress disorder (PTSD) is an anxiety disorder caused by very stressful, frightening or distressing events.

Someone with PTSD often relives the traumatic event through nightmares and flashbacks, and may experience feelings of isolation, irritability and guilt.

They may also have problems sleeping, such as insomnia, and find concentrating difficult. These symptoms are often severe and persistent enough to have a significant impact on the person's day- to-day life.

Causes of PTSD - The type of events that can cause PTSD include:
serious road accidents
violent personal assaults, such as sexual assault, mugging or robbery
prolonged sexual abuse, violence or severe neglect
witnessing violent deaths

military combat
being held hostage
terrorist attacks
natural disasters, such as severe floods, earthquakes or tsunamis"
(Source: NHS website)

Traumatic Brain Injury –Concussion

Even a concussion can cause substantial difficulties or impairments that can last a lifetime. Whiplash can result in the same difficulties as head injury. Such impairments can be helped by rehabilitation; however, many individuals are released from treatment without referrals to brain injury rehabilitation, or guidance of any sort.

A concussion can be caused by direct blows to the head, gunshot wounds, violent shaking of the head, or force from a whiplash type injury.

Both closed and open head injuries can produce a concussion. A concussion is the most common type of traumatic brain injury.

A concussion is caused when the brain receives trauma from an impact or a sudden momentum or movement change. The blood vessels in the brain may stretch and cranial nerves may be damaged.

A person may or may not experience a brief loss of consciousness.

A person may remain conscious but feel dazed.

A concussion may or may not show up on a diagnostic imaging test, such as a CAT Scan.

Skull fracture, brain bleeding, or swelling may or may not be present. Therefore, concussion is sometimes defined by exclusion and is considered a complex neurobehavioral syndrome.

(Source: https://www.headway.org.uk/)

Acknowledgements

Firstly, I would like to honour Red Mountain for his continued guidance and gentle encouragement. My relationship with him has led me to where I am now.

A big shout out to the boys in my life, my husband Rob and my son Dylan. Rob has shown much patience, as I have flitted about from one random job to another - unsure and frustrated with need for money versus my need to honour my souls' journey; often encouraging me to follow the direction and determination of my Spiritual desires.

To my Mum, who has been a constant pillar of strength throughout my life, despite having some very momentous hurdles of her own. This woman has shown me courage, love and strength.

My Dad, for his endless encouragement, to try new things and in his words "give it a go". He has always listened, encouraged and understood my unique way and views on life; never ever judgmental and always on the end of a phone.

My besties in the whole wide world – My friends, Emma, Emma and Lisa, who have always stood right next to me, without judgement. Supporting, listening and laughing. We have been friends since early childhood. My cousins, Kerry and Natalie, for their love and sisterly support through tough times.

And Carrie, who's encouragement got this book to print... It was nearly just a Blog. Thank you!

Lastly, I would like to say a big thank you to the many people I have worked with. The many people I have met on programs and workshops I have delivered. To those that I have Coached and Mentored. The clients I have given readings to. I know that many of you will be reading this book – and I wish to honour you for allowing me to be a part of your journey. Thank you for your honesty, as you have opened up to me and allowed me to connect. To those that have persevered through the uncertainty of their first session and allowed the changes to begin. And to the reader I am yet to meet.

Love & Peace,

Vic.

About the Author

Throughout Nicola's life she has always had an interest in Spiritualism. First Counselling, then Colour Therapy, Reiki Master, Angel Cards, Life Coaching, Tarot, Meditation and Development Circles... Nicola Richardson is on a path of mass personal development.

She believes it is important to share her journey into Spiritualism and to squash the notion that all "Psychics" wear purple velvet and for people to understand that she is pretty *'Down to Earth'*.

Natural Mystic

Down to Earth & Spiritual

E-Book Available

'Tune In' and download the playlist of Natural Mystic

Printed in Great Britain
by Amazon